COURAGE
FOR THE
CHICKEN HEARTED

Humorous and Inspiring
Stories for Confident Living

by

Becky Freeman
Susan Duke
Rebecca Barlow Jordan
Gracie Malone
Fran Caffey Sandin

Courage for the Chicken Hearted:
Humorous and Inspiring Stories for Confident Living
ISBN 1-56292-512-1
Copyright © 1998 by Becky Freeman, Susan Duke, Rebecca Barlow Jordan, Gracie Malone, Fran Caffey Sandin
P.O. Box 2002
Quinlan, Texas 75474

Published by Honor Books
P.O. Box 55388
Tulsa, Oklahoma 74155

INTRODUCTION

A few years ago, several women of varied personalities and backgrounds began meeting together regularly for the specific purpose of "seeding and feeding" each other's confidence. Initially, we met to encourage each other to eggs-ercize the gifts of writing and speaking (or chicken scratching and squawking, as the case may be). We soon discovered we all shared a strong nurturing streak, so we laughingly dubbed ourselves, "Hens with Pens."

Before long, we were not only blossoming in our writing and speaking ministries—we were praying with, listening to, and loving each other through every sort of crisis: from newly emptied nests, to trouble in our henhouses with chicks and roosters, to feeling as though the sky really, truly was falling. After sharing our stories with one another, laughing a lot, and enjoying some wonderful chicken feed at lunch, we almost always left with our confidence renewed.

Not wanting to keep this incredible secret cooped up, we've put our respective beaks together and pecked out this book. As you read it, we are praying that the words will inspire Chicken Littles everywhere to stand up tall, look heavenward, and declare, "Even if the mountains should crumble into the sea, even if the sky really does fall, God will be my strength and confidence."

Becky Freeman
Susan Duke
Rebecca Barlow Jordan
Gracie Malone
Fran Caffey Sandin

TABLE OF CONTENTS

Section I
At Rest in the Nest
Confidence in the Future

Section II
Birds of a Feather
Confidence in Relationships

Section III
Under His Wings
Confidence in God's Love

Section IV
Perched in High Places
Confidence in Overcoming Obstacles

Section V
I Think I Shell!
Confidence in Exercising Gifts and Talents

SECTION I

At Rest in the Nest

Confidence in the Future

CHAPTER 1

Wet Behind the Feathers

by Rebecca Barlow Jordan

It was our first Sunday at the new church. The ink was barely dry on my driver's license, and it would be a year before Larry and I signed the marriage license. Yet here we stood in the great West Texas metropolis of Lillyville, eyeing with awe and reverence our new place of ministry. We were two college students in love, ready to change our world—all 200 people in it according to the last town census—plus a few stray dogs and cats.

"Shall we?" asked Larry. I felt like a timid Moses, trembling before the crossing of the Red Sea. We were a handsome duo— he in his city-slick suit, and I in my sun-yellow coat, hat, and heels. I smoothed some feathery hair strands, wore my best smile, and pushed through the massive church doors. Had we known then what the next few years would bring, we might not have been so eager to cross the threshold.

The church itself sat at the end of a long, graveled road dotted with a few houses, all leaning a little too far to the left. The building looked like something out of a Norman Rockwell painting. It could have passed easily for "The Little Brown Church in the Vale"—with a new white paint job, that is.

The modest church had been adorned with most of the essentials, except for indoor bathrooms. Hardwood floors, a hefty pulpit, a couple of classrooms, and a lone piano that must have belonged to someone's great-grandmother were its meager assets. I sat down to play a few notes and counted seven keys that stuck—estimating the last tuning must have taken place at least 50 years ago. A few dozen wasps flew around the lights, ready to dive bomb an unsuspecting victim in the pulpit directly below. Long, rich, walnut pews lined the church in even rows. And there above the piano hung the monument of monuments: the Church Attendance Banner. I quickly noted the last recorded attendance: Sunday morning: 25. Sunday night: 7.

Just then, a 90-something, feisty, wisp of a woman stepped through the doors. This was our introduction to Miss Gordy. She propped her bony hands on her hips, looked right at Larry and asked him a no-nonsense question: "Are YOU the new pastor?"

"Yes, Ma'am. I guess I am."

"Why, you're just a kid!" she said, creaking across the floor until she found her spot on the back row.

Larry and I quickly gave each other a *what-have-we-gotten-ourselves-into?* look. We were both still wet behind the feathers. I felt totally unprepared for this new leadership role. Even though I'd grown up as a daughter of a minister, I was completely without confidence in this "wife-of-a-preacher" role I was about to play. Miss Gordy wasn't helping matters. She gave new meaning to the term "irregular person," and could easily have won a significant place in *The Guinness Book of Most Unusual Church Members*.

We soon discovered that Miss Gordy took a dim view of "forgettin' the offerin' takin'." If Larry failed to pass the plate at the appropriate time, Miss Gordy would move to the aisle, stand directly in front of the pulpit, and while my husband preached his best Billy Graham sermon, she'd jingle her coin purse until an embarrassed farmer-deacon started the plate around.

Because of our long commute back and forth to school, those dear church people of Lillyville took us under their wing each Sunday afternoon. Mostly farmers, they literally "put on the bird" for us. We dined in converted barns, large ranch kitchens and everything in between. One Sunday we even "caught" our own fish dinner when the host had nothing to feed us. But every cook (including Miss Gordy) stirred up "blue ribbon" fare.

After a year of weekly commutes to the church on the weekends, Larry and I married, and the congregation fixed up the parsonage so we could stay over on Saturday nights. One weekend, we were walking downtown ("downtown" being one restaurant, a gas station, and a faded, red-brick post office) when we heard a loud commotion behind us.

"Look out—Oh, Lordy!" someone yelled. "Here comes Miss Gordy!"

We looked up in time to see our local senior daredevil gunning her 1955 Plymouth in reverse down the old highway—straight toward us and the post office. Even having a disabled forward gear couldn't stop Miss Gordy. We dove for cover and narrowly missed a shower of flying bricks as she backed full speed into the corner of the post office. Nothing— absolutely nothing—deterred this strong-willed widow.

During the three years we stayed at the church in Lillyville, we had an interesting, ongoing tug-of-war with Miss Gordy. She loved to decorate the church with flowers. But the first time we saw her "Bud" (or was it Michelob?) vase perched on the piano, I chucked the bottle (anyone inspecting the trash might have assumed they had a real problem preacher on their hands) and exchanged it for a simple flower vase. The next Sunday her "Bud" vase of flowers appeared again. Realizing we'd never win this battle, we agreed to allow Miss Gordy's novel "Bud" vase a position on the other side of the piano.

But nothing topped the challenge of Miss Gordy's Christmas mission offering—large bills rather than her usual nickels and dimes signaled an exercise in sacrificial giving from her sale of scrap iron. It wasn't until we discovered that tools, plow sweeps, and other farm implements had disappeared mysteriously from community farms that we realized Miss Gordy meant to see that she wasn't alone in her "sacrificin'."

After our years with Miss Gordy, we knew we could handle anything—or anyone, and our confidence grew. Larry conducted his first funeral in Lillyville. I taught my first adult Bible class. We introduced people to our loving Father, and many embraced Him openly. We even completed the church's first building program, which included the installation of venetian blinds and the construction of two *indoor* bathrooms. (Can anyone say "Hallelujah"?) We endured wasp stings, freezing pipes, "no-shows," snores, and so much fried chicken, we thought we'd grow feathers.

Those dear people in Lillyville believed their main mission in life was to give awkward preacher boys a place to squawk and talk their way through college. They offered their homes, their hospitality, their friendship, and a generous $35-a-week salary. They endured the immaturity of a couple of city chickens—kids who didn't know much except that they loved Jesus, and they loved people—even irregular ones.

Maybe that's all that really matters.

*The L*ORD* said to me, "Do not say, 'I am only a child.' You*
must go to everyone I send you to and say whatever I
command you. Do not be afraid . . .
*for I am with you . . ." declares the L*ORD*.*
Jeremiah 1:7-8

Lead? Who Me?

Chicken Nugget

Moses said, "I can't squawk well."
(Exodus 4:10)

Gideon said, "I'm an unknown bird."
(Judges 6:15)

Jeremiah said, "I'm just a baby chick."
(Jeremiah 1:6)

Jonah said, "I'd rather fly the coop."
(Jonah 1:3)

Peter said, "I'm too chicken hearted."
(Matthew 14:30)

Esther said, "What if my goose is cooked?"
(Esther 4:11)

Elijah said, "I'm too pooped to pluck."
(1 Kings 19:4)

CHAPTER 2

Men Are from the Barnyard, Women from the Coop

by Rebecca Barlow Jordan

I ducked my head to avoid the flying rice as we ran down the stairs of the church. As we reached the last step, I looked up, saw the waiting getaway car and bolted to the left, just as Larry bolted to the right. "Get in!" someone yelled. I looked up just in time to see one of my husband's best friends opening the car door for me. He grabbed my arm, and I realized, in sheer horror, I was about to be kidnapped—from my own honeymoon!

I jumped back and glanced over my shoulder. There beside an identical beige Chevrolet stood my new husband waving frantically. "Rebecca—over here!" I ran to him, stumbling over my gown, and sank with relief into his waiting arms. It wouldn't be the last time I'd feel confused in our marriage.

At the tender age of 13, I had already reached my full height of 5 feet 9 inches when an incredible 6-foot, 15-year-old hunk sat down beside me in church. All 100 pounds of me drooled like a frothing puppy. I knew it was a sign from above that he was the one. So what if the seat next to me was the only one available?

Larry and I survived a long teen romance, then headed for college. After my freshman year, we were married on "a wing and a prayer" and rode off on a white horse named "Blissful Ignorance."

The first time we entertained, I proudly set my chicken spaghetti in the center of our $39.95 kitchen table—in my already scorched Teflon skillet. Larry was mortified, but he knew I didn't handle criticism well. So he gently suggested I might want to unpack our serving dishes before we invited company for dinner again.

In spite of my clueless beginnings, we managed to live for quite sometime in what most would call a fairy-tale marriage. The formula was easy. If Larry asked me what I wanted to do, I gave the same safe and inoffensive answer, "I don't know, Honey. Whatever you want to do."

Gradually, I discovered we had some major differences. He sorted; I tossed. He cleaned; I swiped. He filed; I piled. He cut; I ripped. He folded; I stuffed. He discarded; I hoarded. He planned; I schemed. The hall closet served as an unorganized catchall battleground for our differences.

For a long time, I thought Larry had a photographic memory. It was uncanny how he could remember things. I, on the other hand, was always forgetting something. Then he told me his secret: he made lists. *What kind of challenge is there to a system like that?* I wondered.

Then one evening, I was trying to remember an important phone number when Larry asked me his favorite question: "Why didn't you write it down, Rebecca?"

"I did, Honey. On a very important envelope flap."

Larry raised his eyebrows.

"Oh, no, Larry—you didn't! It was right here on the kitchen cabinet, next to those notes I'd scribbled on that paper napkin," I wailed.

"Sorry, Hon," he replied matter-of-factly, "but I think the garbage men just took off with your catsup-stained files."

Traveling together proved to be quite a challenge for Larry, but eventually, he grew accustomed to my pre-takeoff whine of apology, which usually began halfway to the airport: "Honey," I'd begin with a pitiful start, "I think I forgot something."

"What did you forget this time?"

I'd name a half dozen unimportant items: "hair spray, toothpaste, mouthwash, deodorant." He'd roll his eyes with that "not-again look."

"Rebecca," he spoke over my droning, "we're going to be late. Didn't you make a list?"

". . . my PMS medicine," I continued methodically.

"Your what?"

"I also left my PMS medicine." I smiled sweetly.

Larry must have entertained a vision of a mad woman racing through the kitchen waving a knife. Before I could continue, he pulled a Uey, and we would be headed back home to retrieve my sanity-in-a-bottle. We managed to hop on the plane just as they were closing the gate.

Don't get me wrong, we often laughed about our differences. But there were a few times when nothing seemed funny anymore. Fortunately, Larry and I both had parents who made it through tough times together. That knowledge, coupled with God's constant faithfulness to us in the past, helped bolster our confidence that we could find a way to work through our own problems.

By the time we discovered that we had drifted away from each other emotionally, we knew that giving up was not an option. We also knew that counseling was in order. So with battle scars still fresh and a determination to nestle, not wrestle, and a lot of help from God, we embarked on a journey—back to the future. It didn't take long to realize, like the church in Ephesus in the Book of Revelation, we had "lost our first love."

In our mind's eye, we looked again at the screen of lofty dreams and earnest promises— "for better or worse," "for richer or poorer," (lots of "poorer"). We watched in slow motion the instant replay of two scared kids leaving all things familiar and cleaving together to the unknown. We relived both the floods and the refreshing showers, and on the horizon we caught a glimpse, a dim outline, of a multicolored rainbow: a vision of what our marriage could become.

Getting there was another matter! I first had to discard my dog-eared script of "Sleeping Beauty Meets Prince Charming"—and with much prayer, we began the writing of a new chapter in our lives.

As we get older, most of us married couples look wistfully back on our early years of struggle and wish we could have known then what we know now. But life doesn't work that way. God, in His wisdom, knows that struggle—like the butterfly emerging from its cocoon—is an important part of growth and freedom. The things that get stuck in our craw are the very instruments God uses to form our character into Christlikeness. And in marriage, opposites—like magnetic poles—attract each other to the very strengths God knows they need.

Months later we were sitting on the couch, basking in our newfound relationship when Larry leaned over and gave me not a peck, but a long, lingering kiss and embrace. As if awakened from a deep sleep, I dreamily responded with the words I knew my own Prince Charming was longing to hear. "Say! How about we light some candles, turn on some romantic music, and clean out the hall closet tomorrow?"

With a twinkle in his eye, Larry replied gallantly, "Better write it down!"

Many waters cannot quench love; rivers cannot wash it away.
Song of Songs 8:7

Chicken Nugget

Opposites Attack

I'm discovering every now and then,
We're not at all alike;
You want to jog until you drop;
But I prefer a bike!
You like a sense of order,
With nothing out of place;
But clutter doesn't bother me
As long as I have space.
You're a left brain, I'm a right brain;
You like sunshine; I like rain.
You love to clean and organize;
To me? That's a pain!
Perhaps we need to compromise;
Until we find the key,
There's only one thing left to do:
Agree to disagree.

CHAPTER 3

Foxes in the Henhouse

by Fran Caffey Sandin

As I hurried to complete the Saturday morning chores, I waited with anticipation for our date! My husband had invited me to go out that evening—a special treat for any mother of three preschoolers. On this particular day, I felt especially in need of some pampering. That's when I spied the new jar of "oatmeal mask" on my bathroom vanity, touted to stimulate the skin and make it glow like a young girl's.

I turned the lid and sniffed at the mixture. *Hey, why not get gorgeous and get the vacuuming done at the same time*, I reasoned? I patted on an extra thick layer of the oatmeal formula, thinking it would take more than the ordinary dollop to beautify my stressed out and neglected skin. Then, while the children played, I shoved the droning machine back and forth. My face tingled as the oatmeal began to set, and I couldn't help feeling proud of my cleverness. I was accomplishing two important goals at the same time.

I had whirred my way into the last bedroom when, suddenly, I had the oddest feeling that someone was watching me. My back was to the bedroom door when I heard a man clear his throat. I clicked off the vacuum in time to hear his quick and desperate apology.

"Ma'am, excuse me, Ma'am. I didn't want to scare you, but your son invited me in, and I wanted to show you our new line of carpet sweepers."

By then my museum-like expression had set—frozen in time. I couldn't scream, smile, or even say a word. In slow motion, I turned around to face the man, my raccoon eyes peering out of the bumpy plastered mask.

The poor guy grew more startled with each of his goose-steps backwards. "Oh, oh, no, no," his eyes widened as he stuttered, "I—I, think I've made a mistake!" Then he whirled around and headed for the door, dragging his sweeper behind him. Safely outside, he broke into a run and is probably still running today, wondering, *Who was that masked woman?*

As I removed the mask, I noticed that my face was warm and glowing, but I wasn't sure if that was the result of anger, embarrassment, or the wonder-working oatmeal. Then I walked down the hall to have a heart-to-heart talk with our five-year-old. The little guy seemed genuinely oblivious to any wrongdoing.

"Steve," I asked, struggling to control my voice. "How did that man get into our house?"

"He rang the bell and you were busy," Steve replied innocently. "I was helping you, Mommy."

"Son, I realize you were trying to help," I squeaked out in the kindest voice I could muster, "but we don't want strangers walking into our house. Never invite anyone in unless Mommy or Daddy give their permission."

As a mother, I often struggled to maintain my sanity. Our youngsters were active and bright for which I was thankful; but I often felt inadequate for the task. How could I encourage their innocent trust and still teach my kids to be cautious?

"Lord," I prayed, "help me to teach my little chicks to be wise to any foxes that sneak into their lives. But keep them innocent as lambs in Your presence." It wasn't long before a "fox" of a different sort entered our home leaving me unabashedly bewildered.

On the occasion of our ten-year-old daughter's birthday, she received a voluptuous teen-aged doll decked out like a Las Vegas showgirl. I didn't want to hurt the feelings of the child who gave the gift, so I kept quiet while the little girls "ooohed and aaahed."

After the party, my daughter Angie turned to me and asked sincerely, "Mother, you don't like the doll, do you?"

At that point, I didn't know what to do or say, so I flashed a quick silent prayer. *Dear Lord, please give me wisdom. Help me be imaginative rather than destructive. This is one of those delicate situations, and I don't want to blow it.*

"Angie," I said brightly, "bring your doll into the bedroom and let's talk about it." Like two teenagers at a slumber party, we flopped on her bed and propped the doll up on a pillow.

Then I asked casually, "Honey, does anything bother you about this doll?"

She thought for a minute and said, "Well, her outfit is kind of, you know, it just doesn't seem like something I'd want to wear."

"I know what you mean", I sighed. "Kind of skimpy, isn't it? Oh, Angie, there is nothing wrong with having pretty hair or a good figure, but I want you to know those aren't the most important things. A person's character is so much more important. And what we wear says something to others about what's inside of us—don't you think?"

Angie nodded enthusiastically as I continued. "You've been wanting to learn how to use the sewing machine, and I think this is the perfect time. Let's go to the store, pick out some patterns and material, and whip up some beautiful new clothes for this little Miss Priss. What do you say?"

In the days and weeks that followed, my daughter and I spent hours working on the tiny garments. I had to get bifocals, and at times, I wanted to pull my hair out, but Angie was so proud of our designing efforts. While vacationing in historic Williamsburg, we even found a perfectly charming Southern Belle dress to add to the doll's now lavish wardrobe.

Some years later, I was surprised when Angie decided to put her beloved doll in a garage sale. Together, we went through a drawer full of carefully folded doll clothes that we had sewn together. It touched my heart to discover that she had so carefully preserved this symbol of our mother-daughter bonding and the happy hours of informal creativity we shared. "Oh, Father," I whispered, "Thank You for those sweet memories."

Today my children are grown, and I look back with gratitude. During all my years of mothering, I learned one thing for sure. Our God has creative answers for all our mothering dilemmas. Funny. As I think back on those early days, I realize it was often the awkward situations that provided the best opportunities for teaching my children. From the vacuum salesman incident, my son learned to check with me before letting strangers into our home (especially when Mommy is wearing breakfast cereal on her face). And from a barely clad plastic doll, my daughter learned that part of being a beautiful girl means dressing creatively, fashionably, and modestly.

When we mothers ask Him, God is extraordinarily faithful to help us handle all life's little foxes—be they man or molded plastic—that creep into the henhouse.

*Catch for us the foxes, the little foxes that ruin the
vineyards, our vineyards that are in bloom.*
Song of Songs 2:15

Pattern for Living—
One-Size-Fits-All Guide

Chicken Nugget

I. Material Required:
    Love, joy, peace, long-suffering, faith,
    goodness, gentleness, meekness, temperance

II. Notions Needed:

Elasticity	Forbearance
Variety	Lip Zipper
Sense of Humor	Backbone Stiffening

III. Measurements:
    How wide is your understanding?
    How long is your patience?
    How deep is your love?

CHAPTER 4

Feeling All Cooped Up!

by Becky Freeman

I sat on the couch nursing Baby Gabe, turning pages of *Pat the Bunny* for my toddler, Rachel, and motioning for my oldest sons, Zach and Zeke, to stop wrestling so near the coffee table.

My mother, who had dropped by for a visit, spoke up over the din of her karate-kicking grandsons. "Becky," she began, "I know that it feels like these years of buckling kids in car seats, and pulling car keys out of the potty, and wiping your $50-an-ounce perfume off the kitty cat will never come to an end. But really, Sweetie, one day you'll look behind you—and no pairs of little feet will be following in line. They'll be at school. Or at college. Or married. Or on the other end of the phone line asking you to baby-sit the grandkids."

"Oh, mother," I started to say, "that reminds me. . . ."

"So sorry, Sweetie," she interrupted as she rose to take her leave, "I've got to run. I have an appointment to get my hair and nails done before the ladies luncheon at noon."

I watched, squirming with escalating envy as my manicured mother kissed the grandbabies good-bye, walked calmly out the door carrying one and only one bag (her purse), opened one and only one car door (the driver's side), and buckled in one and only one tummy (hers). *Will I ever again see MY day of freedom?* I pondered. *I'm penned up by four miniature guards with peanut butter on their faces. Some days, I'd love to fly away from this coop!*

I have to admit the Kids-At-Home-All-Day Decade was a long one. But these days, when I pass a peanut butter-covered toddler, some part of me always winces with nostalgia, and sweet memories of my own babies come racing back through time. Today, my peanut-buttered toddlers are peanut-buttered teenagers. (At least now they make their own sandwiches and clean up after themselves.) Now I'm the woman with hair and nail appointments. I drive and buckle-up solo. I meet women friends for lunch with nary a thought of crackers, tippy-cups, or high chairs. I speak, for the most part, in complete sentences.

I also look back with compassion and gratitude to the mother of multiple preschoolers I once was. I wish I could go back in time, hold both of her dishpan hands in mine and say, "Thank-you. You are doing the right thing. Not one moment will be wasted. Every hug you give, every diaper you change, every lullaby you sing, every Dr. Seuss book you read for the ninety-seventh time, every prayer you pray at the end of an exhausting day is worth it. Oh, so worth it. If only I could show you what I know now. If only you knew how quickly the 'little kid' days disappear, and how soon the 'big kid' days will arrive to take their place.

"You will hang in there—sometimes by a delicate thread—but you'll finish this Great Tricycle Race. And at the finish line, four wonderful, capable, loving 'big kids' will be waiting to thank you—or, more realistically, to ask you if they can borrow the car keys. But there are small blessings even in this: at least you don't have to fish the keys out of the commode. Your teenagers will take the keys, give you a quick peck on the cheek, and drive off with your prayers and a boulder-sized chunk of your heart, but hey, you'll have your freedom again!

"Only you'll have to wait for the car to get back in the driveway to use it."

I was driving to Mother's Day Out one day when I heard Kay James speaking on a radio show about how really long and varied a woman's life is. In truth, the majority of our years will be spent without the responsibility of children in our homes. Through misty eyes, I jotted down notes and fragments of what she said and to this day, I try to keep these thoughts ever present as I meander through these few remaining years of childrearing.

"Every woman juggles many things," Mrs. James said. "Now some of the balls we juggle are rubber—they can be dropped and will bounce back at a better, later time in our lives. However, some of the balls we are juggling are crystal. Delicate, priceless balls, they cannot be dropped and picked up later on. They break quite easily. Our children are those magnificent balls. Please don't drop them during the years they are in your care; let the bounce-back kind go instead."

Then she said one other thing I've never forgotten, "Yes! A woman can have it all—she just can't have it all at once. There are times and seasons for everything in a woman's life."

To you mothers out there who are struggling through days of diapers and dolls and dirty handprints on walls, I applaud and encourage you. You are the true heroines of womanhood. Be of good cheer, there will be more freedom in your future. Briefcases, put on hold, will come out of the closet, all dusted—once again into service. Your gifts and talents that, for now, must be tended in haphazard, short, and stolen moments, will have their season to flourish into full bloom. A few short years ago when the highlight of my day was nap and cookie time, I never dreamed that I'd be writing and traveling and speaking to hundreds, even thousands of women. And it is fun, fun, fun.

But I will never do anything as important or meaningful as rocking a baby, taking a meandering walk with a toddler, or hugging a hurting child who needs his mommy. John Whitehead once said, "Children are arrows we send into a time we will not see." Giving our kids focused attention during their formative years will not only help them be loving, giving adults, it will affect the course of history for generations to come. What calling or corporate career could possibly top that?

There is a time for everything, and a season
for every activity under heaven.
Ecclesiastes 3:1

Chicken Nugget

Top 5 Ways to Spot a Mother Hen on a Date

1. She immediately moves all salt, pepper, and sugar packets out of arm's reach.
2. She reaches in her purse, pulls out a baggy of Teddy Grahams, and offers them to her husband as a pre-dinner appetizer.
3. She gives her order to the waiter in baby talk. "Is the pasta that twisty around and around kind, or the itty-bitty baby snail shell kind? Because the twisty around and around kind tastes really yucky."
4. She stands up and tucks her husband's napkin under his chin. Then she returns to her seat, folds her napkin into the shape of a diaper, and lays it in her lap.
5. Before leaving the restaurant, she asks her husband, "Are you *sure* you don't need to go to the potty? It's a thirty-minute drive home now."

Thanks to the MOPS Group at First Baptist Church, Richardson, Texas, for your input on this nugget!

CHAPTER 5

Your Chickens Will Come Home to Roost

by Susan Duke

One of my most vivid childhood memories is how my mother used pet phrases to teach us kids life's lessons and points to ponder. Recently, my sister and I wrote a long list of all the ones we could remember and laughed until our sides hurt. We can always make tears of laughter roll down Mama's face when we remind her of the maxims we heard on a daily basis. Once when I was a teenager, I wrote her a letter using as many of her epigrams as possible, hoping to sway an unfair decision I thought she had made. She laughed at my wit and applauded my motives but never wavered in her decision.

One phrase I remember hearing most often was, "Your chickens will come home to roost," often followed by "you mark my words, Suzie, one day they will!" I never quite understood what my mother meant; I just knew it didn't sound good! I could only assume that one day I'd be old enough to find out.

After becoming an adult and having children of my own, I found that Mama's words, indeed, took on a profound clarity.

Although I'm not proud of it, I must admit, on occasion I'd embarrass my mother in public. It was usually in an innocent, humorous way, but it still left my mother red-faced and flustered. Like the Sunday—I was about four years old—when suddenly I was filled with the urge to belt out a song with the rest of the congregation. While the others softly sang, "Amazing Grace," I climbed boldly atop the church pew and sang a song my older brother had taught me— "Hey Joe, Where'd You Get That Pretty Girlie?" My brother, who couldn't contain his outburst of laughter, had to be led outside by our Mama Hen whose Sunday feathers had been seriously ruffled.

Strange how this particular chicken "came home to roost" years later while sitting in a Wednesday evening church service with my own daughter, Kelly.

Midweek service was generally reserved for a time of prayer. Kelly, a junior in high school at the time, was normally quiet and reserved in the church setting. As the pastor asked for those who had a prayer request to raise their hand, I watched curiously as Kelly lifted hers and waited for her turn to speak. When called upon, she earnestly offered her request.

"I would like to ask everyone to pray for a friend of mine who is really going through a rough time. She is going into the hospital tomorrow morning to have a vasectomy."

For a moment there was nothing but stunned silence. When it became obvious that I, The Mother, had been silently elected to correct my daughter's indiscretion, I very gently took her hand and said, "Honey, you mean hysterectomy."

My normally quiet daughter, raised her voice and sharply retorted, "No, Mother, I mean vasectomy!"

Again, as demurely as possible, I repeated my previous statement, tagging on an extra clarification. "Sweetheart, men have vasectomies and women have hysterectomies." Convinced this would halt any further discussion, Kelly unpredictably turned downright indignant. She insisted she knew exactly what she was talking about. Snickers, held in restraint, now burst forth helplessly from all over the church. Red-faced and fighting to keep his composure, our pastor proposed, "Well, whatever the problem, we know we need to pray. Let's all kneel at our seats and bring these requests before the Lord."

At that point the laughter came roaring down the aisles like Niagara Falls, washing away any hope of saving grace. Out-and-out hysteria reigned. As I caught glimpses of others on their knees, shaking, bobbing, snorting, hee-hawing, and wiping away tears, my own embarrassment gave way to bellows of laughter. The pastor couldn't pray, and the church sounded like a barn full of braying donkeys. Why, if anyone had walked in at that moment, they'd have thought revival had broken out.

The prayer service was cut short that evening—but we all left with our prescriptions filled by the good medicine of laughter. Needless to say, it was a Wednesday night that made history in our little church. However, I must add, this would not be the last of my chickens that would come home to roost.

Kelly, my beloved chick, now has a daughter of her own. But even as an adult, she continues to use words in ways that leave us all helpless with laughter. Recently, I overheard my tenderhearted child passionately telling her husband, "Oh, Robert, I could never eat an artichoke's heart!"

As with so many of the things our parents told us, I discovered Mama's clichés turned out to be true. You really shouldn't count your chickens before they hatch. And all of your eggs really ought not go in only one basket. And most assuredly, "Your chickens will come home to roost!" Her words have been marked and will remain forever safe and sacred—roosting within my heart.

A man hath joy by the answer of his mouth: and a word
spoken in due season, how good is it!
Proverbs 15:23 KJV

Mama Always Said . . .

Chicken Nugget

Don't count your chickens before they hatch,
Don't kick a dog when he's down,
Beauty is only skin deep,
What goes around comes around.

Every cloud has a silver lining,
Every dog has his day,
Don't judge a book by its cover,
Save for a rainy day.

Don't put all your eggs in one basket,
A stitch in time saves nine,
Practice what you preach,
Make hay while the sun shines.

You can lead a horse to water,
But you can't make him drink,
Two wrongs don't make a right,
You are what you think.

Count your blessings every day,
And fill your life with love—
For every gift we're given
Comes from the Father above.

CHAPTER 6

Roosting High (On a Hill)

by Fran Caffey Sandin

"What are we going to do?" I asked. "We've got to find a place to live!"

As a new bride, I was eager to build a little nest of my own—to use all our pretty wedding gifts, and finally, to settle in. Unfortunately, everything we had seen was either too expensive or too far from work. As we drove along the streets of Little Rock, Arkansas, our tail feathers were visibly dragging.

"Well, let's look through the newspaper one more time," Jim suggested.

"Good idea!" I responded with all the cheerfulness this tired chick could muster. "I saw a coffee shop just a few blocks back."

Jim wheeled our old Oldsmobile around, and we chugged to the diner. My sweet husband grabbed the newspaper, opened the door for me, and with long, serious faces, we walked inside the "barely in business" eaterie. After adjusting to the stale aroma, we found a booth near the back where Jim folded out the want-ad section one more time.

As we sat side by side, sipping steaming coffee and scanning the newsprint, my eyes landed on a new ad.

"Look, Jim! It says 'Furnished apartment. MUST SEE TO APPRECIATE'—and here's the address. What do you think?"

"We have nothing to lose—let's check it out."

We finished our coffee, and walked out the creaking café door with a new strut in our steps. After four days of looking, we hoped this would be "the place."

As newlyweds, just returning from our honeymoon, we never dreamed finding a place we could afford would be so difficult. Jim had just graduated from medical school and I from nursing school. We were anticipating his yearlong internship at the medical center and I planned to begin working soon at the University Hospital. But for now we were, shall I say, "financially challenged." In fact, we were hauling everything we owned in a 5' x 7' U-Haul trailer. Our worldly goods may have been meager, but we were both rich with families who loved us and encouraged our faith. So we prayed, in childlike trust, for God's guidance.

As we drove up to a lovely white two-story house, just a few blocks from the medical center, I kept reaffirming the address aloud. "Could this possibly be right? Yes, this is it!"

While parking our car, we noticed another couple getting out of their pickup from across the street and walking toward the house. *Oh dear*, I thought, *they must have seen the ad, too.*

Sunshine highlighted the perky red geraniums in the front flower boxes as Jim and I held hands and walked to the door. A smiling, middle-aged woman greeted us as I inquired, "Is this the apartment advertised for rent?"

"Yes, please come in," the lady spoke graciously. "I'm Mrs. Ratcliff. Another couple is looking, too, but you're welcome to take a tour."

Mrs. Ratcliff explained, "My mother lived here but she passed away a few months ago. I don't want to stay upstairs by myself, so I decided to rent out this bottom floor as an apartment."

As we walked through the well-kept, spacious home with high ceilings, I gazed at the nice dining room set and started to cry, thinking, *This place would be just perfect for us!* (Poor Jim. He was bewildered. Our roosters don't understand that we chicks cry *joy tears* as well as sad ones.)

The gracious owner continued guiding us through the home. "I'm leaving everything as is—washer and dryer near the kitchen, TV in the living room, and all the furniture—including this antique bedroom suite."

We were still looking and talking with Mrs. Ratcliff when (thankfully) the other couple decided not to take it. They left. We stayed.

In the course of conversation, Mrs. Ratcliff found out we were newlyweds. I was almost afraid for Jim to ask about the rental fee, but when she told us the price (with bills paid), it turned out to be about half of what we expected—well within our budget. Still dabbing at my eyes, I looked at Jim and he looked at me. Then we both turned toward Mrs. Ratcliff and, in unison, announced, "We'll take it."

I was so eggstatic, I felt like cackling all day! God had guided us to this wonderful abode—and it was even perched high on a hill. The view was beautiful. But there was another reason our hilltop perch was a special blessing.

Our old standard transmission car needed a new battery and, of course, we couldn't afford one. With our new home, all we had to do to get the car started in the mornings was to roll down the hill, pop the clutch, and away we'd go! Worked like a charm.

Jim and I had different work schedules, but the house was so convenient to the hospital that all I had to do was don my boots and start walking. I enjoyed many walks in the snow on my way to work. Not only was our location convenient, Mrs. Ratcliff ended up adopting us into her heart, and even named her downstairs apartment "The Honeymoon Cottage." She would occasionally knock at the door and hold out a batch of freshly baked cookies. For our first Christmas, she presented us with a Christmas tree skirt—which we still use.

Each year when I unpack our decorations, I am reminded of God's love and how He guided us to our first home. Sometimes we forget that our Father loves to give good gifts and even eggstra treats to His children. He is always watching over us, like a Mother Hen, keeping us roosting near His heart.

And the LORD will continually guide you,
and satisfy your desire in scorched places.
Isaiah 58:11 NASB

Chicken Nugget   Mrs. Ratcliff gave us a plaque and I've found its message to be true:

"LOVE WORKS IN WAYS THAT ARE WONDROUS AND STRANGE, AND THERE'S NOTHING IN LIFE THAT LOVE CANNOT CHANGE."   (Author Unknown)

CHAPTER 7

Feed Sack Dresses

by Gracie Malone

When weathermen in Texas predict a "cold front," it may mean the temperature is about to drop from a sizzling 101 degrees to a merely blazing 95. On the other hand, it could mean a drastic plunge of 30 degrees or more. When you factor in the high humidity levels, our weather is more than unpredictable. It's downright confusing.

Deciding what to wear is one of life's biggest challenges for any chic Texas chick.

In the weather-iffy month of September, I spent the night with my grandchildren. Early the next morning I began fluttering about the bathroom, getting ready to make a mad dash back home to Greenville to lead a women's Bible study group.

That my life is one mad dash is an issue often discussed at our house. Our son Mike was eight when he shook his head and solemnly said, "Mom, you sure live life in the Vaseline!" (Of course he meant "in the fast lane.")

Either way, my wheels are well-greased, and my gear is usually in "Drive." That's one reason I've worked hard to simplify my wardrobe. After years of experimenting, I've pretty much narrowed it to one option—blue denim—although I do have outfits in various shades of light, medium, and dark indigo.

Since the forecast warned of a possible cold front, I had packed two options—a dark denim number with long sleeves and a light denim outfit with short sleeves. Before I could choose my attire for the day, I wanted a weather report from a truly reliable source. I bellowed down the hall, "Anybody been outside this morning? How's the weather?"

Six-year-old Connor, just in from the backyard, yelled back, "It's not very hot, but, it is. . . ." He paused a few seconds as he searched for the right word, then loudly pronounced, "It is humidiated."

I laughed as I opted for the short-sleeved outfit, then I pondered Connor's confident manipulation of the English language. Why, if he can't think of the right word to use, he invents one of his own that's even better. "Humidiated," in my opinion, is far superior to "humid." I, too, fret over words, and sometimes when I get stuck, well, like Connor, I create one that "suitifies" me—much the way I've found that all-purpose denim "suitifies" my personality and lifestyle.

On the drive home I smoothed the wrinkles in my skirt and thanked God for denim—the state fabric of Texas. We wear denim to rodeos, picnics, theaters, baptisms, weddings, and—set off with the right black velvet vest—denim can even be worn to a formal affair. I enjoy the confidence I feel when I get dressed to go out. It hasn't always been so.

When I was a kid, sometimes on Saturday I would get up early, put on an old pair of jeans, climb into Daddy's pickup truck, and accompany him to his weekend job at the Lancaster Feed Mill. There I spent hours racing around grain silos, climbing on bales of alfalfa, or lounging on bags of chicken feed. Sometimes I made change for the customers while Daddy loaded their trucks from the dock. And he always paid me two nickels—one to buy a Coke from the shiny new machine and another to buy a peanut patty from the big glass jar on the counter. Then, as I munched the sweet snacks, I wandered through the bags of feed selecting fabric for my back-to-school dresses.

In those days no one had to give us lessons on recycling. Almost everything we bought served multiple purposes. Feed sacks were made of sturdy cotton material—reusable fabric with colored dots, bright checks, or cute country prints. At our house they provided the basic raw material for cup towels, aprons, quilt squares, pillowcases, mother's "house dresses," and my cute little pinafores.

I felt pretty when I wore my homemade creations to school and church—until the day I noticed what the other girls were wearing: soft pastel dresses, plush velveteen jumpers accented with pearl buttons, corduroy skirts with white blouses and crisp lace collars. As I compared my clothes to those of my friends, my self-confidence plummeted. I wanted so badly to please my parents so I never complained. But deep in my little chicken heart I longed for just one store-bought dress!

I was a chubby preadolescent before I finally got my wish. It started with a family shopping trip to Levine's department store. Together Mother and I sorted through the racks until my eyes fell on a lovely dress the color of chocolate milk with whipped cream. I wanted—no, I was dying for—that dress. But I knew when Daddy curled his lips and said, "Oh, no, not *brown!*" that it was not to be. To please him I picked out a red dress decorated with white daisies and garish yellow rickrack. (Cheap, cheap, cheap!) The next Sunday I felt like a country bumpkin version of *The Ugly Duckling* as I waddled into my Sunday school class. There sat the rows of pretty girls in their delicate Easter outfits with bonnets and white gloves to match. I felt, to borrow a word from my grandson, totally "humidiated."

By the time I reached my teen years, I came to an important decision. I would dress to please myself. My dad wanted me to look like a Rhode Island Red, but I was a feisty Brown Leghorn trying to break out of her shell. Color wasn't our only battleground; length also became a source of conflict. My mom cringed one day when I donned a pair of brown short shorts and strutted through our living room when the Baptist preacher was visiting.

Eventually I learned how to handle my dad. When I wanted my way, I'd curl up next to him on the couch and tease, beg, and badger until he cried for mercy, or reached for his pocketbook.

Fortunately, as I matured into a young woman, I also grew in my relationship with Jesus Christ. I began to feel loved and accepted by Him. As I focused on spiritual growth, my appearance didn't seem as important. Rather than finagling my way with Dad or setting my mother up for a shock, I simply relaxed and gained confidence in who I was in Him. That confidence filtered down to every area of my life—even to what I wore.

Today, with a little planning ahead, I could afford a dress made of velvet and lace. Funny thing—as it turns out—the soft ultra-feminine stuff isn't really "me" after all. And I'd rather be chicken-fried than caught in short shorts. Just give me a classy ensemble in denim, and I'm not only in blue-jean bliss—I'm the sassiest chick in town.

Man looks at the outward appearance,
but the LORD looks at the heart.
1 Samuel 16:7

Top 10 Best-Dressed Chicks

These famous hens are recognized for their
fashion achievements this year.

Chicken Nugget

1. *Little Red Hen* is awarded the *Tri-Color Ribbon* for wearing colors that compliment her skin tones.
2. *Big Fat Hen* wins the *Creativity Award* for her ability to conceal figure flaws.
3. *Henny Penny* gets the *Penny-Pinchers Prize* for saving money on her wardrobe.
4. *Ducky Lucky* receives a *Cash Prize* for finding special outfits in outlet malls.
5. *Chicken Little* receives the *Award of Excellence* for looking good in short shorts.
6. *Goosey Loosey* takes the *Merit Prize* for her comfortable casual clothes.
7. *Foghorn Leghorn* receives the *Golden Cornucopia* for sportin' textured leggings and boots.
8. *Turkey Lurkey* wins the *Blue Ribbon* for being "tastefully dressed" for the holidays.
9. *The Ugly Duckling* is awarded the *Medal of Honor* for her remarkable improvement in personal appearance.
10. *Mother Hen* wins the *Loving Cup* for wearing her old dresses one more year so she can buy cute outfits for her little yellow chicks.

CHAPTER 8

Mid-Hen Crisis

by Becky Freeman

Sometimes I look at myself in the mirror and think, *Not bad for a 39-year-old chick.* Other times I look in the mirror and wonder, *Who let that ol' goose in the henhouse?* Being smack in the middle of midlife reminds me a lot of my middle school years when I was too old to be a cute little kid, and too young to be a key-carrying, free-wheeling teenager. I lived in kid purgatory for a few years there. Now I'm in middle-aged no man's land: too old to be considered a young chick, too young to be a wise old hen.

You know who I envy these days? Surprisingly, it is not the Cindy Crawford-types posing on covers of magazines. No, the women I envy look more like Barbara Bush. I'm looking forward to the old hen stage—when my age will fall closer to the national speed limit. Here in the middle ages, it is becoming such an effort to keep up appearances. My makeup bag bulges with under-eye concealer, feather-proof lip liner, and a multitude of wrinkle erasers. My new skin lotion sounds like a name for a sorority house: Alpha Beta Hydroxy Complex. (With microbeads no less. I don't know what they do, but they sound impressive, don't they?) I can't wait to be far enough away from youth that I can legitimately throw in the antiaging towel and get on with growing good and old.

How well I identify with these lines from Judith Viorst's book, *Necessary Losses*.

I'm working all day and I'm working all night
To be good-looking, healthy, and wise.
And adored.
And contented.
And brave.
And well-read,
And a marvelous hostess,
Fantastic in bed,
And bilingual,
Athletic,
Artistic.
Won't someone please stop me?

Who decided we had to try so hard to stay young? I love those happy clusters of silver-haired women you see exiting from tour buses. The kind whose very attire and demeanor says, "Who cares? I'm over 70 and I'm entitled." The sort who have memorized the poem, "When I Am Old I Shall Wear Purple" and embraced its philosophy into their lives and wardrobes. When an 80-year-old woman wears orange stretch pants, a purple polyester shirt, Nike tennis shoes, and a hot-pink visor, folks call her "fun-loving" and "young-at-heart." But we of the pushing-forty crowd would be labeled something altogether different if we donned the same "fun-loving" ensemble. I say that it's reverse age discrimination!

The over-70 age group also gets lots of financial perks—like Medicaid and a cheap cup of coffee at McDonalds. On the other end of the spectrum, the under-seven age group also fares well in the penny-pinching department: little kids are always being given free stuff—balloons and candy and toys in their kiddy meals. But markdowns or freebies for "in-betweeners" are nonexistent. When was the last time you saw a sign that read "Middle Age Discount"?

I've been thinking about this disparity for awhile, and as a result, I have a dream, a new vision for change. Remember that Million Man March on America's capitol a few years back? Well, I think we ought to organize a Middle-Aged Women's "Waddle on Washington" in a collective effort to make our society more midlifer friendly. I've even written a speech outlining the changes I'd like to see.

If I, a woman of the middle ages, were in charge of the country—

Donuts would be declared a health food.

Walking into a room and forgetting why you are there would be a sign of genius.

Men's pajamas, sized extra large, would be considered elegant evening wear.

Glasses and car keys would holler, "Right here!" when you ask aloud, "Where did I put them?"

The word "plump" would be interchangeable with the word "sexy" and "attractive."

Everyone would agree to always be late to everything. (This way, you see, we'd all get there at the same time. I don't know why people in charge don't consult me on these things.)

And, if I were in charge of the country—

There'd be a generic name—like maybe, "Harry"—that could be substituted anytime you forget the actual name of the dear, lifelong friend you are talking to.

If I were in charge of the country—
Wrinkles on faces could be starched and ironed.
Twenty-year-olds could take your aerobics classes for you.
Teenagers would always be asking, "What else can I do to help you, Mother?"
If I were in charge of the country—
On long car trips, husbands would be required to periodically ask their wives, "How would you like to stop at that cute little gift shop, have some tea and scones, and shop for an hour or so?"
A sense of humor and a kindhearted nature would be valued more highly than being skinny or young or beautiful.
The End

If we could somehow manage to get these few items changed, then the word midlife might not be paired so often with the words like *crisis* or *crazies* or *malaise*. Instead, we'd hear maturing women announce, "I'm in Midlife Bliss." Or "I'm at that ol' Midlife Prime—I love my life and I like who I am. God is good."

Come to think of it—I *am* in love with my life. I *do* like who I am. And God is good. Even at 39 and holding.

Maybe we ought to hold off on that Waddle to Washington for awhile. For even though our midlife bodies are a little baggier here and there, these mid decades can actually be the most fulfilling of our life. I recently heard a man say, "I think women have this incredible 'blossoming thing' happen when they turn 40. They get an extra boost of confidence or something, and it's like they suddenly say, 'Look out world! I'm coming out of my shell!'"

I think he may be right. But before I hatch out of my middle-aged shell and go take over the world I have one last important question to ask:

"Does anybody remember where I put my car keys?"

They will still bear fruit in old age,
they will stay fresh and green.
Psalm 92:14

Crowings on Growing Older

Chicken Nugget

"Of course, at 17 you wonder how anyone over 30 breathes on their own."

K. T. Oslin

"Midlife crisis is that moment when you realize your children and your clothes are about the same age."

Bill Tammeus

"My signature is holding up, but sometimes I almost forget what my name is. I look down as I sign and I think, *Is that right? Is this me?*"

Lauren Bacall

CHAPTER 9

I'm No Spring Chicken Myself!

by Gracie Malone

One morning we decided to visit "Mama," my 103-year-old grandmother who lived in the nursing home. I settled in the car's back seat next to Mom as my sister Lois climbed in front with Aunt Grace. Feeling good, I closed my eyes to bask in the sunshine and listen to the older women folks chatter.

I opened my eyes when my 84-year-old mother started fumbling through her purse. From the depths of her bag, she retrieved a shiny surgical-steel instrument and polished it with her hanky. I wondered what she was doing until suddenly I recognized her tweezers. Without one word of warning, my mother took aim, and plucked my chin. She proudly displayed her prize: one curly, half-inch-long, silver hair. Her mission accomplished, Mom replaced the tweezers in a tiny leather case and deposited it back in her purse without missing a beat in her conversation.

As I rubbed my chin, I realized, *One sure sign of growing older is you lose hair up top and it sprouts in the most bizarre places.* Peering over my aunt's shoulder, I examined my face in the mirror and wondered, *was Mama my age when she got her first clipping?*

For several miles, we discussed the peculiar problems of those who are, well, "chronologically gifted." Mother said that as you get older your ears get bigger and your nose grows longer. I guess it's God's warning signal that from here on out your basic five senses are going to need help. I've noticed how older folks get "hard of hearing," but, do they also get "hard of smelling?" And, even though we tried, we couldn't think of a single good reason for sprouting a lone hair on one's chinny-chin-chin.

At a recent hen party I was talking to an old friend seated next to the window. I couldn't help but be distracted by an inch-long gray hair growing right out of a wrinkle on her cheek. Now that I think about it, I'm thankful I didn't have any tweezers to take care of the situation.

Before we reached our destination, I pondered my own aging process—an issue I'd struggled with recently. I suppose I'm coming to terms with my mortality. To be honest, I'm chicken about getting old. During recent years, I've ducked a midlife crisis, plunged headlong into the empty nest syndrome, and now, just as I'm winging my way toward liberty and leisure, I'm in a flap about senior citizenship.

At the nursing home, Mother slipped her arm in mine as we walked down the long corridor, and into Mama's room. Standing by her bed, I felt overwhelmed by my grandmother's frail form barely visible beneath the sheets. *Mama's lived entirely too long, I thought. Why doesn't she give up? Why doesn't God take her on home?* But, soon my perspective changed.

Like a hen hovering over her brood of chicks, my mother fluttered and fussed over Mama. She washed her face with a warm cloth, brushed her hair, and applied lotion to her gnarled hands. I overheard Mother clucking tenderly, "Everything's okay. I'm here. I love you, Mama." My heart melted as I thought about my rich heritage from these two women, and suddenly 103 years didn't seem enough.

Days later, my fear of the future faded as I read, "He who dwells in the shelter of the Most High will abide in the shadow of the Almighty. He will cover you with His pinions, and under His wings you may seek refuge; His faithfulness is a shield and bulwark." I thanked God for His promise to those who love Him: "I will set him securely on high. . . . With a long life I will satisfy him, and let him behold My salvation" (Psalm 91:1,4,14,16 NASB).

I got a visual picture of Mama, my mother, and me, huddled together under God's wings like three old wet hens in a storm. I imagined the warmth and security I'd feel snuggling in the soft feathers close to the heart of God, feeling every heartbeat. Just the thought of it was enough to make this chick feel safe and confident.

The next weekend, I checked into the hospital for mini-surgery. Since I'll probably live an eon, (if genetics have anything to do with it) I decided to take care of my health. The procedure the doctor performed was, in my opinion, nothing short of a miracle. Through a tiny incision he removed all the stuff I didn't need, then using a little camera, with flash attachment, he took pictures of everything I had left.

At my next appointment, the doctor proudly displayed 8 x 10 glossies of my innards. As he pointed out my "inward parts," I felt apprehensive. He tapped one picture with his pen and said, "This is your liver." He sighed, clicked his tongue approvingly, and with deep appreciation in his voice, added, "What a fine liver!" When I'm feeling uneasy, just one little compliment can make my day—*any* kind of compliment.

As I left the doctor's office and strutted toward my car, I kept repeating in a giddy voice, "I have a *fine* liver. I, have a fine *liver!*" I not only felt healthy, I felt internally gorgeous all afternoon.

I suppose most of us women are chickenhearted about one thing or another. But, it doesn't take much to make us feel confident. With just one word of kindness or a simple compliment, we sprout wings and fly. So, next time we hens are gathering, let's squawk about things that are friendly and nice.

If we can't think of anything kind to say, we can at least try this: "I'm sure you have a lovely gizzard."

And, puhleeeeeze, keep your tweezers in your purse!

One generation shall praise thy works to another,
and shall declare thy mighty acts.
Psalm 145:4 KJV

Gracie's Forever-Young Egg White Facial Mask

Chicken Nugget

Cleanse face with cold cream and warm water.

Separate one egg, reserving the white in a small bowl.

Apply egg white to face with fingertips. Watch your peepers and beak—(avoid eyelids and lips).

Let the mask dry thoroughly without picking or pecking.

Carefully peel to remove impurities, blackheads, and dry skin.

Rinse face with cool water to tighten pores.

Optional Final Step: Check for facial hairs in daylight with magnifying mirror. Gently pluck with your own tweezers.

SECTION II

Birds of a Feather

Confidence in Relationships

CHAPTER 10

Hens and Neighbors, Gather 'Round

by Fran Caffey Sandin

"Mom," my daughter had told me, "you might really enjoy using a round brush when you blow dry your hair. They're great for adding body and bounce." Since my medium-length hair is an odd combination of thick and fine, I was open to suggestions.

The next time I went grocery shopping, guess what? I was thrilled when I found a cute, small, round brush, for the discounted price of 99 cents. Since I love a good bargain and could envision my hairstyle undergoing a glamorous transformation, I grabbed the beauty tool from the marked-down basket and hurried home to give it a whirl.

As soon as I walked into my kitchen, I plopped down the bag of groceries, turned on the radio and began humming. While putting cans away in the pantry, I ran across my new purchase and thought, *I wonder how this brush works?* Right where I stood by the kitchen counter, I reached up, grabbed a bunch of hair from the top of my head, and tucked the strands into the bristles of the tiny brush. Then I began winding. And winding. And winding—while musing, *Hmm, this is just like rolling spaghetti on a fork.* I was amazed at how many turns I could make.

But I was even more surprised when I discovered the brush that had so beautifully wound up my hair, now refused to let go. I flew into the bathroom, hoping a mirror would help me see a way to release my locks from the evil contraption. I pulled and tugged in all directions. My efforts only succeeded in tightening the tangles. My chicken heart skipped a beat as I imagined being stuck with this bonehead attachment forever—like Pebbles from the Flintstones!

Then I remembered my hen friend, Gracie, who lived only a few blocks down the street. Quickly, I dialed her number. When she answered I stammered, "Gracie, are you my friend?—my *really good* friend?"

"Sure," she said reassuringly, "what's wrong?"

"Well, is it okay if I come over—like, right now?"

"Yes, but what's the matter?"

"You'll know when you see me." When I hung up the phone, I felt a combination of urgency and relief. I ran out the door, jumped into the car, and raced toward Gracie's house like some hair-brained woman.

Considering my delicate condition, I was hoping no one would see me. But while rounding the corner, my hopes were dashed. There stood a rather dignified-looking lady in her designer jogging suit. As I drove by, there was little I could do but smile and wave at her. From my rearview mirror I watched her head slowly swivel in my direction, a look of shock rising on her face. I tried to reassure myself, *Maybe she'll think I'm starting a new trend—"brush-roll-n-go."*

The minute I pulled up to Gracie's sidewalk, she flung open her front door and immediately began laughing. Stepping out to meet me she asked, "What have you done to yourself?"

I didn't know whether to laugh or cry so I scooted inside, closed the door and blurted, "Help! Gracie, this is serious. What am I going to do? I cannot get this brush out of my hair! I have pulled and jerked in every direction, but the brush keeps on taking wrong turns. Can you work on it? Please? I know you can do it. I have confidence in you, Gracie. Please."

"Well, let me get the scissors," Gracie quipped with a twinkle in her eye.

"Oh no! That's what Jim would do."

After a pause of playful hesitation, Gracie said, "You poor, pitiful chick. Have a seat at my kitchen table."

Gratefully, I scooted my chair into place as I fondly thought, *Gracie and I have shared many cups of tea and talked each other through so many ups and downs around this table.* Now here I was in the middle of yet another situation I simply could not handle without my friend and neighbor.

With the tender-loving care of a mother hen, Gracie began the arduous task of unwinding the mess of matted hair, strand by strand. Though it sometimes hurt when she pulled, I didn't dare squawk or cackle. A little pain was better than the wig I'd have to buy if this operation proved unsuccessful. After 15 or 20 minutes of concentrated effort, punctuated by outbursts of laughter, Gracie triumphantly declared, "TA DA!"

Then she sang out, "Here's your lovely hairstyling accessory," as she showed me the brush. It looked like a hamster that had been caught in a whirlwind.

I grabbed the beastly brush and asked Gracie, "Where's the nearest trash can?"

Thankfully, only part of my hair stayed with the bargain brush. I touched the top of my head and found some remnant. Breathing a sigh of gratefulness, I gave Gracie a big hug and promised I would "be there" if she ever needed me to do anything. Ever. At all.

Later as I reflected on my emergency I thought how thankful I was to have Gracie as my neighbor. What would I have done without her? Then I began thinking about how important it is for us to reach out, especially to those who live around us.

Before the days of air-conditioning, folks spent time on their front porches, often chatting with their neighbors. Most activities revolved just around the church and the school instead of the myriad of "extracurriculars" which now bombard us. Hens had quilting bees; roosters helped each other build fences and barns. Now, in our mobile society and insulated houses, we have to make an extra effort to get to know our neighbors.

Sometimes I am so busy with my own "to-do" list, I fail to be a good neighbor. But when I do take the time, it helps me capture warm feelings of community. I begin to have compassion for the struggles of others. There are so many ways to show concern. Sometimes all it takes is a telephone call, stretching a recipe to have an extra plate of warm, homemade goodies, or even just sharing a good book.

My brush with "the brush" taught me just how important it is to develop relationships before a crisis occurs (not to mention buying a large round brush). No matter how independent we think we are, there'll be times when we desperately need someone who cares (and is even willing to "de-brush" our hair).

Love your neighbor as yourself.
Matthew 19:19

Chicken Nugget

Hens and Neighbors

Would you like a cup of coffee
Or perhaps a cup of tea?
Dear Hen Next Door
Please take time to notice me.

When I need a soft shoulder
Or should you need mine,
We'll choose flexibility,
Leave those "Organizers" behind.

I promise to come a struttin'
If ever you should shout.
Rest assured I'll be there
If your feathers all fall out.

CHAPTER 11

Adult Chicks of Fairly Functional Hens

by Becky Freeman

They sit on our shoulders and cackle in our ears, even when they're a thousand miles away. At times you can't live with 'em, but there are moments when it seems you can't possibly live without 'em. Even the best of them hurt us at times; and the worst of them seem to manage to come through for us occasionally. Who? Our mothers, of course.

Since my mother is also my close friend, my original writing teacher, and co-author with me of our first two books, people often assume we are completely in sync in our thinking. Not so. Remember, our second book was called *Adult Children of Fairly Functional Parents*. Mother and I each have our own unique set of quirks.

Still, in many ways, I am like my mother. We laugh at the same things, enjoy lingering over lunch at the cafeteria, chat about the trivial, and philosophize over the meaning of life. We both cry at romantic movies and triumphant chorales. We both lose our car and experience the emotional moment when we finally find it in crowded parking lots. Once, after trying on clothes in a dress shop, my mother accidentally tucked her skirt into the back of her pantyhose and ended up "mooning" the entire mall. On a recent shopping trip, not to be outdone by my mother, I found myself in the same embarrassing predicament and "mooned" all of Wal-Mart.

However, with all of these similarities aside, the older I get the more I realize that, though I am definitely my mother's daughter, I am not her clone. I remember well the day I decided to declare my own independence and establish my own personhood.

Mother and I were moving through the line at Luby's cafeteria, when I brazenly overlooked the gooey fudge desserts and reached for a bowl of plain egg custard. Mother stopped and placed her hand over her heart as she struggled to recover from the moment of abject betrayal.

"We don't like egg custard in our family," she finally managed to say. "It's bland. It's plain. It tastes like scrambled eggs with sugar in it. It's for dull people with ulcerated stomachs. We—you and I—are strong, chocolate-nut women!"

Now how's a daughter to argue with that? Since I had come this far out of the Plain Vanilla closet, I decided to charge recklessly ahead. "Mother," I swallowed hard. "I've been wanting to tell you this for a long time. Please try to understand. You were bound to find out someday. And I might as well be the one to tell you. I also like—tapioca pudding."

Bewilderment clouded her eyes, but though taken aback, Mother has always tried hard to be a "with-it" kind of mom, wanting to support us kids in all of our decisions. Eventually she even joined me in sharing a bowl of bread pudding. Sure, she doused hers with a generous dollop of fudge sauce, but it was the thought that counts.

That day opened up a continuing dialogue about the gradual but profound changes taking place in our relationship—without either of us really realizing it. When our mother-daughter relationship expanded to include professional writing, my confidence in my own abilities gradually began to increase. Today I am actually teaching, mentoring, and doing professional editing for other new writers. Still, I wondered if my mother would ever come to see me as a fully functional adult.

One day soon after my cafeteria declaration, she called to check on the time of our next get-together. Just before signing off she said, "It's going to be raining. You'll need a raincoat, you know." Then catching herself being a mother hen she said, "Oh, dear, there I go again."

"Mother, it's okay," I reassured her. "I am a big girl, but I know you're just trying to show me you care. In small doses, it's kind of nice to be mothered. Every once in awhile."

"Oh, well," she sighed, " I might as well go ahead and say this too. Don't forget to go potty before you leave."

Obviously, this friend-equal concept was going to require a little reinforcement. When we met again for our regular lunch date, I seized the opportunity to assert myself once more. As we were finishing our spinach salads, the waitress walked by pushing the beverage cart.

"May I get you anything? A cup of coffee, perhaps?" she inquired. I waited to be sure I had Mother's full attention and then spoke with deliberate casualness.

"Yes, I'd like a cup, please." From the corner of my eye, I saw Mother sit straighter in her chair, as if she had been poked in the back by an invisible finger.

"You don't drink coffee," she said in amazement. "You don't even like it!"

"I know," I replied in my most professional voice. "I'm making a unilateral decision to enjoy some anyway. I love holding the cup and savoring the aroma—makes me look mature and sophisticated, don't you think?"

She swallowed hard before answering. "Come to think of it, it does!" Then she smiled a wicked smile, lifted her own cup to mine in a toast and added, "Careful, don't spill! It's hot."

We may as well give up and accept it: the shadow of a mother's wings are never far from her chicks—no matter how old her babies get or how far they fly from the barnyard.

But speaking the truth in love, we are to grow up in all aspects.
Ephesians 4:15 NASB

(Much of this chapter is excerpted from *Adult Children of Fairly Functional Parents*, copyright © 1995, Broadman & Holman Publishers.)

Ruthie Arnold, speaking of her mother (and Becky's grandmother), Nonnie.

Chicken Nugget

"We had very little in this world's goods, but we did have our mother. Sometimes her 'gems of wisdom' echo through my mind as if she were standing just behind me as I live my life even yet."

CHAPTER 12

Marching to the Beat of a Different Drumstick

by Gracie Malone

When hens flock together, somebody is bound to ruffle a few feathers. It happened recently when my good hen friend, Carolyn, met me at a conference in Dallas. During the morning break, we were discussing matters of eternal significance when we noticed an elaborately dressed and coifed woman clicking her heels in our direction. Carolyn stepped backward, grabbed the handrail, and from the corner of her mouth muttered, "Brace yourself!"

Within seconds the feisty hen settled her way into the space between us and started clucking, "Oh, Carolyn dahling, I miss you soooo." Carolyn opened her mouth to speak, but the hen kept on squawking, "I do think about you often, why, I think about you every time I see you!" With that, she spun on her high-heeled talons and headed off to greet a nearby gaggle of geese.

Carolyn was stunned. "What did she say? 'I think about you every time I see you?' Is that another way of saying, 'Out of sight out of mind'?"

Later we had a long talk about how our unbridled beaks get us chicks in trouble. At one point I declared, "Sometimes I talk so fast, I say things I haven't even thought of yet." From there, Carolyn and I launched into a discussion about the variety of hens in our gatherings, then on to how we cope with difficult people.

I have to admit that some of my acquaintances fall into the "difficult" category simply because they are different. We're a mixed brood of southern belles, Yankees, city-slickers, country bumpkins, Protestants, Catholics, and Jews all struggling with crossing cultural barriers.

Hailing from opposite sides of the Mason-Dixon line, Carolyn and her husband Jim couldn't even agree on what to have for supper when they were first married. When she served Texas corn bread and black-eyed peas, he'd tease, "Hon, in Minnesota we feed those things to the cows." And to this day, when her brother-in-law, Bill, heckles her about "chiiicken friiied steak" she wants to clobber him with the skillet. (By the way, Jim's been converted. Now he gobbles whatever Carolyn puts on the table—including the "cattle feed.")

We not only have unique backgrounds, but different gifts, talents, experiences, personalities (and personality disorders) that set us apart. The other day when I visited my friend, Vern, we discussed that very thing. She poured coffee, set a plate of cookies on the table, and with a mischievous grin, plopped down a napkin that read, "Let's put the fun back in dysfunctional." I said the first thing that popped into my head. "Oh, those kids of mine. . . ." When I finished my tales, Vern responded with stories in kind.

Vern has taught me a lot about loving people (including our kids) just as they are. If I could just love everybody like Vern loves them, like Jesus loves them, I'd be more at ease when the occasional odd bird waddles into my corner of the world's pen.

Vern is one of those people who invites me to simply be myself. Maybe it's the thirty-minute drive from my house in Greenville to hers in McKinney that helps me relax and let my guard down. Maybe it's the way she listens without shaking her head or clucking her tongue. All I know is that as soon as I put my feet under her table, I'm ready to talk about everything that's bothering me. And, if I just happen to expose a character flaw, a lousy attitude, or personality quirk, I know Vern's one chick that's unflappable.

Everybody needs at least one Vern.

The more we learn to love each other, the easier it is to accept our differences. And it's important to realize that we can accept, without having to understand each other. The Lord never told us to figure everybody out. He just said, "Love." My own husband can't even understand me. In fact, I once told him "Joe, just stop trying to figure me out. Even if you could understand me, you wouldn't believe it."

Joe is not the only bewildered rooster in the barnyard. One evening my friend Carol was reading the Bible while her husband Lowell rested nearby. With her finger on a verse from First Peter, Carol paused and asked sweetly, "Lowell, what does it mean to 'live with your wife in an understanding way'?" Lowell, who's an expert at things theological, stretched, groaned, and with furrowed brow, droned his answer. "I . . . have . . . no . . . earthly . . . idea."

At one time or another I guess all of us have to deal with a peculiar someone. We can't understand them, so they're hard to love. When this happens, we just have to forgive. In a grocery store the other day I observed an incident that brought this truth to mind with new clarity.

Patsy, a friend of mine, was standing in the grocery aisle comparing fat grams on cans of chicken soup when one of life's oddest ducks, let's call her "Goosey Loosey," rounded the corner and headed her way, chiffon scarves just a flyin'. Patsy visibly cringed. "Sue," Goosey began as she took Patsy by the arm, "How in the world are you? And don't you look absolutely gorgeous this evening?"

I moved behind a display of cookies to see how Patsy would handle Goosey's addressing her by the wrong name. I also happened to know Sue, and though Patsy and Sue look somewhat alike, there are some important differences.

Patsy, usually a mild-mannered chick, exploded in an outburst of defensiveness. "Look, quit getting me confused with Sue! You're always getting me mixed up with her. Sue is fatter than I am!" So there! Patsy had said something she'd obviously wanted to say for a long time.

I couldn't take my eyes off the unfolding drama. Her feelings made known, Patsy tugged on her rumpled sweatsuit and waddled off toward the pasta section.

For a moment, Goosey looked stunned. I let out an audible gasp when I saw her floating toward Patsy again, chattering all the way. The eternal fixer-upper, this Goosey on the Loosey, was sure she could clear everything up with a few more words of explanation.

"Oh, Honey, Oh, Patsy!" she chimed in a voice that could be heard 'round the store. "You're not fat. Why, you're not nearly as fat as I thought you were. You're skinny, I mean, you're little. I mean, you're *just the right size!*"

Patsy spun around and squawked, "Look, I am fat. I know I'm fat. I know exactly how fat I am. But I'm not *as* fat as Sue!"

Ah, me. Situations like this call for liberal doses of forgiveness among hens.

At least until we learn when to keep our "tongues in chick."

When words are many, sin is not absent,
but he who holds his tongue is wise.
Proverbs 10:19

A Prayer
(Author Unknown)

Chicken Nugget

Lord,
Keep me from becoming verbose and
possessed with the idea
that I must express myself on every subject.
Release me from the craving
to straighten out everyone's affairs.
Teach me the glorious lesson that
occasionally I may be wrong.
Make me helpful, but not bossy.
With my vast store of wisdom and experience,
it does seem a pity not to use it all—
But You know, Lord,
I want a few friends at the end.
Amen.

CHAPTER 13

Fine-Feathered Friends

by Susan Duke

One soul-searching evening, my husband Harvey and I made a drastic decision that would forever change our lives. We decided to leave the big city and fulfill our lifelong dream of moving to the country.

It was a tough decision for several reasons. First of all, we hated leaving our dear friends and home church. It was especially hard to leave my business. For years I'd owned an antique and gift shop in a suburb of Dallas; I loved my work and grew to love my customers as well. Often they'd ask me to come and decorate their homes for them. In the process of doing so, we'd usually move beyond a decorator-employer arrangement to a client-friend relationship.

I was an "eye-ball-it and make-it-work" kind of decorator. Once a customer named Vicki called me in tears.

"Suzie," she cried, "can you help me? I hired an exclusive decorator from a furniture store, and my house is now in the biggest mess. I just phoned the store and asked them to take everything back. Help! Please!"

Like a doctor answering a house call, I drove right over to help re-feather my client's nest—"Suzie-style." The first thing I decided to do was hang a large framed print over her sofa. I held the picture up to the wall, eyeballed it, then sat it back down and as I took aim at the nail with my hammer. "Wait!" Vicki exclaimed. "You didn't measure! What if that's not the center of the couch?"

"Then we'll move the couch," I replied matter-of-factly. We enjoyed a laugh and went on to create a cozy nest she and her family would enjoy for years to come.

Some decorating ventures proved more egg-citing than others. For example, I once went to decorate the home of a builder in a prominent neighborhood. To reach the top of a 12-foot kitchen wall, I climbed a tall ladder. Then I stood at the top, nail in hand, preparing to hammer an antique advertising sign above the sink. As soon as the nail was in place, I heard the strangest hissing sound, followed by a gush of water.

Suddenly fire detectors started beeping and alarms began shrieking throughout the house. The phone rang, and before I could climb down the ladder's slippery wet steps, I heard the shrill of sirens and tires screeching to a halt in the driveway. It was the fire department and the police, poised and ready for action.

Within minutes, the bewildered builder and home owner arrived at the scene. When they traced the source of the problem to my little nail, which had punctured a copper pipe behind the wall, I couldn't believe it. How could one tiny mistake create such havoc?

Once the area was cleared and my customer graciously reassured me everything would be fine, we enjoyed a few hearty cackles. That crazy experience actually laid a foundation for a warm and long-lasting friendship.

Selling the business, our home, and moving to the country proved to be more than a simple adventure in relocating the family. Little did we know we would be embarking on the most trying and faith-deepening experience of our life. Through the trials and adjustments to life in the boonies, our career-oriented goals gradually became replaced by a simple and intense longing to know God in more meaningful ways, and especially to find His purpose for our lives. This search eventually led into a full-time speaking and singing ministry.

Then one day I received a phone call that delighted my heart from a person out of my past. It was from a client/friend named Cheryl, whom I hadn't heard from in years.

"Suzie!" she exclaimed, "You'll never believe what has happened to me. My whole life has changed."

Cheryl had been one of my favorite customers. From the start, mutual admiration and trust had characterized our relationship. When her newly built home was finished she'd asked me to decorate it in the same country style I'd used to adorn my own home. Cheryl's home was frequently used for entertaining, so I always took special care in finding pieces and accessories I felt were suited to her unique lifestyle, personality, and taste. Enthusiastic and bubbly, she always seemed overjoyed with my selections. I assumed her reason for contacting me now would be related to business, but this was to be more than a casual reacquaintance call.

"Suzie," Cheryl continued, "believe it or not, I'm calling to ask if you'd come and hold a Bible study for me and several of my friends. Would you be willing to come one day soon?"

Pleased, but somewhat shocked, I told Cheryl I would call back in a few days to set a date. As I gently hung up the receiver I thought over the days when Cheryl and I worked all day decorating her home, breaking only for lunch. Always there was plenty of laughter, but often our conversations would turn from superficial chit-chat to deeper searchings of the soul. Even then, I had sensed a spiritual hunger in Cheryl that was longing to be fed. True to my word, I phoned Cheryl back and told her to get ready. I was coming to share from the scriptures—"Suzie-style."

The 50-minute drive to her home in the city gave me time to pray and reflect. "Lord, what do You have in mind for today?" I asked as I glanced heavenward. Knowing Cheryl was new to the Christian faith, I had prepared a basic Bible study, wanting to leave plenty of time for sharing and prayer. As I turned a corner, a simple but profound thought occurred to me: *God never wastes anything. He will take the most insignificant events, bringing them forth into new light, and use them for His glory—just as He is doing now.*

The study was held at Berta's home, a mutual friend of Cheryl's and of mine. Berta had also been a client during my "decorating years." We found a place to relax in the warm and comfortable den. I recognized an old blue quilt, made in the 1800s, that Berta had purchased from my shop to hang over a cupboard door. A wreath I'd embellished still graced her mantle. I felt honored that these women were now trusting me with a much greater task than accenting their homes. As we opened our Bibles, read aloud, and shared, I could almost feel my heart smiling. Awed that this special moment was taking place because these ladies had happened upon my little shop many years ago, I thought, *God, as long as I live, I'll never be able to figure You out.*

I concluded our time together with a prayer of thanksgiving. When I looked up, my eyes met Cheryl's. A steady stream of tears rolled down her cheeks. Her voice strained through sobs as she spoke. "Suzie, I just realized something precious. All those times you came to decorate my house, you were really decorating my soul."

Now I was the one wiping away tears.

I'm not an antique dealer anymore, but I have discovered a wonderful truth: God is. He is in the business of taking old pieces of our lives, refinishing them and, at just the right time, surprising us with newfound beauty.

Always give yourself fully to the work of the Lord,
because you know that your labor
in the Lord is not in vain.
1 Corinthians 15:58

Chicken Nugget

God Is an Antique Dealer

God is an Antique Dealer;
He looks for that which is broken.
He searches in unlikely places,
where pain is the language spoken.
What others view as hopeless junk,
He sees as priceless treasure.
Beneath the layers of brokenness,
where love heals beyond measure.
So carefully He sands the grain
where life's rough edges mar,
And then He pours His healing balm
into every well-worn scar.
With grace He seals His masterpiece.
What beauty He beholds!
Yes, God is an Antique Dealer—
He deals in restoring souls.

CHAPTER 14

Building a Nest Egg of Memories

by Rebecca Barlow Jordan

Even when we were grown, my mother usually sent one of us kids home with a special treasure—a delicate china cup, a collector's ornament, a favorite book, or even a check to help with school expenses. And always, she made sure her gifts were divvied among us equally and fairly. We could almost hear her mental calculator clicking away: Let's see—two dolls equals one antique pitcher; five books equals two pillows; one plate of cookies equals three bottles of pop. I rarely, if ever, felt she treated any of us with partiality.

I didn't fully realize Mom's influence until we had children of our own. Christmastime each year usually raised my inner red flag of fairness. "But I spent $75 on one daughter and only $74.50 on the other," I would say to Larry. "Maybe I can find a 50 cent gift for her stocking." Of course, I'd discover a darling $2.00 bargain instead, which meant another trip to the mall to equal the other daughter's amount. The game continued, until each Christmas I would inevitably exceed—sometimes double—our agreed spending limit. "But, Honey," I pleaded, "I had to spend the same on both girls. I wanted to be fair!"

Treating children equally is ideal, but not always possible. Sometimes all we can do is pray for God to blossom our children in their own unique gifts and personalities—asking for His help to steer them in the right direction, cluck happily after each success, and nurture them through each failure.

A pamphlet I read about poultry said that chickens love to scratch around in the dirt and cover their feathers with dust— to protect themselves from annoying insects. I spent equal amounts of time on my knees and outside my children's bedroom doors "feather-dusting" both of them with mama hen's prayers for protection. Purposely, I tried to avoid the Isaac-Esau, Rebekah-Jacob-type favoritism I had read about in the *Old Testament*. In addition, I wanted my brood to feel the same love from their earthly parents as Jesus has given to me—equally, to all His children.

But in spite of our best efforts, what mother hasn't heard at least one of these accusations? "Mom, where are *my* baby pictures?" "When did I take *my* first steps, and how tall was I in first grade?" Actually, neither one of our daughters can complain about my keeping their books unbalanced. Well, okay, like most parents, we did photograph our first child a little more often—but both of their baby albums show equal amounts of empty, fill-in-the-blank pages. I was relieved to discover that at least I did record that our girls were born. "Not to worry!" I assured them, when they questioned the bare spots in their books. "I'll tell you stories, and then you can build your own *nest of memories*."

And so I have kept my promise. At their college graduations, I presented each daughter with personalized notebooks—overflowing with anecdotes and tales about their childhood. One of my favorite stories gives a glimpse into a lesson God taught me about parenting them fairly, dividing time and attention as equally as possible—perhaps one of the hardest areas for us moms to keep in balance.

My oldest daughter, Valerie, then an eager kindergartner, had asked if we could make an outdoor tent for our dog like the one she had seen in a schoolbook. I said yes and decided to combine the project with one of her favorite pastimes—nature walks. I read off the list of things we would need to complete the job: an old blanket, two sticks, and some string to construct our tent. Since we had no sticks, she and I took off to find some wood in the alley behind our house—leaving little 2-year-old sister, Jennifer, at home with Dad. A quick trip netted us one broken broom handle and several large twigs to use as tent stakes, along with a few other goodies—sticks, smooth rocks, broken chain links, a chipped marble, the remains of an empty bird's nest, and the most surprising of all—money! On the way back, I had glanced down at the fence and spied something that looked like green paper folded up under some dead oak leaves. We parted the leaves with our shoes and discovered two green one-dollar bills.

Later, as we spread our "loot" on the kitchen table, I glanced at my youngest daughter. With her thumb tucked between parted lips, she was standing on tiptoe, wistfully staring at her sister's treasures. *Me, too?* her brown eyes seemed to implore.

The next day while Valerie was at school, I took Jennifer by the hand and asked, "How'd you like to take a treasure walk, too?" We headed for the vacant lot behind us and gathered rocks, played a guessing game of "I spy something God made," and dropped several "treats" into our sack—a chicken feather, a butterfly wing, and the shell of a shiny, green beetle.

Once again, returning to the house, I saw a bit of green peeking out near the edge of a wooden fence. *No Way!* I thought.

Yet there it lay—another crumpled up dollar bill. My thoughts flew to the heavenly manna God sent the children of Israel as they wandered in the wilderness. I was puzzled by this strange occurrence, but pocketed the money—and with much gratitude. Our checkbook's balance had registered a mere $1.59 that morning.

Then Jennifer and I walked back home and added our treasures (both the ones from nature and the ones from our national treasury) to the overflowing bird's nest on the table. The next day I awoke early, as anxious to hit the alley as Jennifer was—on still another hunt. I didn't want to miss finding a single heavenly phenomena. It was a beautiful, crisp day. Red and gold leaves of autumn flew under our feet while we eagerly sifted the ground. This time, however, I scoured the ground not for feathers or sticks, but kept my eyes pealed for some more green "manna bucks" to fill my bank account.

We found no monetary treasures that day. But years later I can still picture my daughter as a young toddler, cheeks pink from the warm sun, her tousled, blonde hair flying in the breeze—and that proud grin on her face as she displayed her week's collections alongside her big sister's trophies.

With a little prodding from above, I'd found some beautiful and lasting treasures that week, ones that God has nestled deep in my heart for a lifetime, ones that no money could ever buy—even the green manna kind.

I'm hoping my daughters will overlook the empty pages in their albums, or at least be willing to exchange them—for stories, that is—stories about two little daughters who grew into two lovely adults, both of them equal in the hearts of their parents.

The other day, while sifting through my own "memory nest," I ran across a sealed envelope—no name on it. When I opened it, out fell five of my daughters' baby teeth. Let's see . . . maybe I could glue these into their baby albums. If I divide these teeth equally—and cut one in half. . . .

Store up for yourselves treasures in heaven. . . . For where
your treasure is, there your heart will be also.
Matthew 6:20-21

Chicken Nugget

Full-Nest Syndrome

The children are gone, but my nest is full
Of pleasant memories and happy times,
Of messy mud pies and warm puppy dogs,
Of favorite bedtime stories and shared dreams.

My nest is filled with fragments of rusty
Bikes and splintered skateboards,
Term papers and frantic deadlines . . .
Pieces of broken dreams and romances,
Of emergency trips and close calls;

Temper times, of heart-to-heart talks,
And shouting matches . . .
Of warm hugs and wet kisses;
My nest has twigs of joy . . .

Like oceanside vacations and frilly dresses;
Bats and balls and pretty dolls,
Threads of laughter and tears,
Of sorrow and fears . . .

Fervent prayers and anxious moments
Hoping, and waiting together.
There's no empty nest here—
My nest is filled with love.

CHAPTER 15

Real Eggs

by Susan Duke

"I'm so egg-cited!" I burst through the door singing a chickenized version of an of old Pointer Sisters song. It was our first writer's group hen meeting after hearing the news that a publisher wanted our book. We weren't just "egg-cited," we were "egg-nited!" We laughed, we talked, and I spontaneously sang a reprieve of this soul song to my chicken soul sisters.

A few months before I would have never let my fellow hens see this zany, crazy side of me, reserved only for close friends and relatives. These outstanding hens were not only new friends, but also my mentors and fellow writers. As the "rookie chick" of the group, I wanted them to see how serious I was about writing. So I was careful not to show my crazy, fun-loving side too soon, for fear they might label me shallow, flip, immature, scatterbrained, or just plain silly.

At first, outside of our monthly "Hens With Pens" meeting, my life only occasionally crossed paths with the other hens. But when we decided to write this book as a group, our "togetherness" increased measurably. We were now joined at the feathers, wing to wing. Most of us have had at least one teary spell where the other hens hovered, offering hugs and a box of tissue. As I laid my soul bare in the pages of my writing and continued to find acceptance, I knew I had found a sheltering coop where I could safely let my feathers down. We were becoming real.

At one of our regular hen meetings, we each brought little gifts for one another. I brought everyone a mini-chicken teapot; Becky gave us all chicken coasters; Gracie purchased sticky notes; Fran presented us with a chicken cake; and recently, Rebecca brought each of us a decorative hen-sized egg in a nest. After handing out white eggs to the other hens, Rebecca smiled as she handed me mine last. "And here is yours Susan," she said with mischief in her eyes, "the only brown egg."

At first I didn't understand. "Why are you giving me the brown egg?" I asked. "Am I the black sheep or something?"

She laughed as she explained, "No, it represents how you embrace and cross those denominational and multicultural barriers in your ministry."

I have to admit, I do love a soulful song and I always include a lot of black Gospel in my musical repertoire. I revealed my passion for soul music the day I told the hens about Aretha Franklin. Though I grew up listening to Aretha Franklin, Gladys Knight, and Patti Labelle, I went through a period in my life when I thought I had to give up listening to anything that I could not find in a Christian bookstore.

Through some maturing, I discovered God's grace crosses many barriers and that a good love song is just that—a good love song. Let's be frank: Julio Iglesius, Kenny G, or an old classic love song sets a much better mood for a romantic candlelight dinner with your husband than does "When the Roll Is Called Up Yonder." (I can hear some of you cheering me on!)

So, I no longer make excuses—I love Aretha!

After speaking one night to a group of ladies at a local church, we concluded our evening with a covered-dish supper. During a casual moment, our conversation turned to the dreaded chore of housecleaning. I told all the ladies, "Hey, I've found a way to make housecleaning almost fun."

"How?" they asked, their eyebrows raised with interest. "Tell us your secret."

"Well, it's really simple: I put a pot of Marmalade Simmering Spice on the stove, stick a CD of Aretha Franklin in the stereo, and can I ever *clean* house!"

Although I spoke candidly, I had no idea anyone would take it to heart—until one morning, about a month later. While putting away dishes in my kitchen, I heard a knock at my back door. I wasn't expecting anyone, so I was surprised when I saw the familiar face of my friend Charlet, who is also the pastor's wife at the church where I had spoken. She never dropped by without notice, so her sudden appearance alarmed me.

"Good morning Suzie," she began. "I hope you don't mind my dropping by without calling first. I was on my way into town, and when I got to your road I decided to take a chance on your being home."

"Is everything okay?" I promptly asked.

"Oh, yes, everything is fine. I just wanted to chat for a minute if you're not too busy."

I assured her I had the time to visit, and I put on a fresh pot of coffee. As we sat at my kitchen table, I filled our cups, still curious about Charlet's reason for stopping by. We talked for nearly half an hour before shy and reserved Charlet finally worked up the courage to tell me why she had really come.

"Do you remember when you were at the church last month, and we were all sitting around talking about cleaning house?" she asked meekly.

"Well . . . yes," I answered cautiously.

"You said something about cleaning house with Aretha Franklin." She continued. "Well, this may sound silly, but I was wondering if maybe I could borrow that tape."

"Charlet, you've got to be kidding. You want to borrow my Aretha Franklin tape? Now remember, it has some pretty get-down stuff on it! What will Pastor Ken think? He may never let you associate with me again if you take this home!" I contended with a broad grin.

She chuckled as she replied, "Oh, it will be fine. I won't play it when he's around. I just need some help to get my house cleaned. If Aretha can motivate you, maybe she can motivate me."

I watched in wonder as the mild-mannered pastor's wife went on her merry way home to let Aretha work her motivational magic.

Whenever I think of Charlet listening to Aretha's "Natural Woman," "Dr. Feelgood in the Mornin'," or "Respect Yourself," I get tickled. Almost every time we see each other, we have a good-hearted chuckle over Aretha's influence in our lives. We are truly soul sisters now. Perhaps pastors' wives most of all need to hear that it's okay to be yourself, be real, and even have a little fun cleaning house!

The more I think of it, the more I like my brown egg. Thanks, Rebecca, for giving this fair-haired chick permission to be my *real* soul-sister self!

*Each one should use whatever gift he has received to
serve others, faithfully administering God's grace
in its various forms.*
1 Peter 4:10

Be Yourself

Chicken Nugget

It's sometimes hard to just be yourself,
Fearing you won't measure up to someone else,
You try to find confidence—try to fit in,
But you are not like every other hen!
So you let down your feathers, dare to be real,
And with bold assurance, share what you feel.
What joy and peace, when you finally realize,
God made you unique—to Him you're a prize!
So remember these words, and whatever you do,
Don't ever feel chicken to just be you!

CHAPTER 16

One Old Hen and Three Little Grandchicks

by Gracie Malone

As grandkids Luke, 6, Conner, 4, and Mary Catherine, 15 months scurried about, I suddenly felt weak in the knees and wondered, *Can I really do all this?* Matt and Rebecca, our son and daughter-in-law, planned a trip to Bar Harbor, Maine, and I, being a gracious grandmother, volunteered to watch over their brood while they were gone. When I arrived, Rebecca explained the kids' schedules, including car pool, soccer practices, and two games.

The next morning, Matt and Rebecca flew the coop, the chicks hopped out of their nests, and the escapades began. During the next five days, I mastered some coping skills, which I now offer to parents and fellow grandparents with my blessing:

1. **Just say yes.** On Tuesday Luke had soccer practice. We scarfed down TV dinners, located his gear, and were heading for the door when Luke bellowed, "Wait, I need to take some water!"

No problem! Mary Catherine had removed that water bottle from the cabinet and I'd put it back in at least a dozen times. I fumbled through the shelves, but it was gone.

"Where's Luke's water bottle?" I yelled. Luke and Connor shrugged their shoulders and helplessly turned their palms up. Mary Catherine grinned. Then Luke seized the opportunity to get something he wanted.

With a voice as smooth as creamed chicken soup he asked, "Grandma Gracie, since grandmothers are supposed to spoil their grandchildren, may I take a Coke?"

I hesitated, then answered, "Grab one for everybody!" Three happy kids and one gullible grandmother flew out the door and landed at soccer practice just in time.

2. **Take mega-vitamins.** Wednesday Matt phoned with a simple request: "Mom, I need my identification badge. Would you send it by overnight mail?"

The next morning after Luke left for school, I found Matt's badge, put it in an envelope, helped Connor buckle up in the backseat of the car, buckled Mary Catherine in her car seat, loaded the stroller, and drove to town.

After 20 minutes, I located the post office, parked, and unloaded. Connor unfolded the stroller, while I unbuckled Mary Catherine and secured her in the stroller. I took Connor's hand and managed to get them lined up inside. After 10 minutes of waiting, I learned that Bar Harbor is "off the beaten path," so mail could not be delivered overnight.

Back outside the post office, I undid everything I had just done: unstrapped the baby, buckled her snugly in the car seat, helped Connor buckle up, folded the stroller, loaded it back in the car, and decided to drive to Federal Express. After all, things should move quickly in a place with "Express" written on the door.

Once there, I decided to forego the stroller. I hoisted Mary Catherine onto my hip, grabbed Connor's hand, and trudged inside. Plopping Mary Catherine on the counter, I started filling out the required forms. She grabbed my pencil. When I moved her dimpled hand, she crumpled the papers. Clearly needing a change in strategy, I put Mary Catherine on the floor next to Connor and pinned her to the counter with my spraddled legs.

"What's your return address?" the clerk asked. For the life of me, I couldn't remember my son's address. "How 'bout the phone number?" Noticing my blank look, she handed me the directory. But, before I could find the right page, the clerk shook her head and said, "Lady, your baby is walking out the door!"

I whirled and ran. As Mary Catherine reached the sidewalk, I swooped her into my arms like a chicken hawk snatching a baby chick. Mary Catherine grinned. Obviously, I needed the stroller after all.

With Connor in tow, I went back to the car, unfolded the stroller, secured the baby again, marched back into the office, and finished the paperwork. Then I loaded the kids, drove home, put my feet up, and popped a handful of vitamins.

3. **Never argue with a 6-year-old.** On Saturday morning Luke's soccer game was scheduled on field 6. Rebecca had carefully pointed out that the kids would not be playing on their usual field. If only she'd explained this to Luke.

On the parking lot before I could unfold the stroller, Luke shouted, "Grandma Gracie, this is the wrong field."

"The schedule listed field 6," I answered confidently.

"But, we always play on that field!"

"Well, today it's 6. Your mother said so."

"But," Luke countered, "my coach said field 5."

My feathers bristled. "Luke, you're wrong. Now get to field 6!"

As Luke trudged across the parking lot, I overheard him grumble, "Well, I believe my coach!"

When we rounded the corner, Luke spotted his teammates on field 6—just as I said. Before he darted onto the field, I just had to make a point. "Luke, were you wrong?"

He shifted uncomfortably, kicked the dirt, and said, "I think my coach was wrong."

I was ready to concede defeat, when he tugged on my sleeve and sweetly added, "I'm sorry, Grandma Gracie."

4. **Realize you can't do it alone.** Each evening I bathed the kids and dressed them in soft pajamas. Then we huddled on the bottom bunk for stories, hugs, and prayers.

Before "lights out" on our last night together, Luke quoted the verses I'd helped him memorize from the Lord's prayer. "Give us this day our daily bread. . . ." As he spoke, God seemed to be listening nearby.

I whispered, "Lord, You are my daily source of strength and wisdom. Thank you for being faithful." Just as I prayed for His guidance as a mother, I sought it even more as a grandmother.

When Luke finished his prayer, Mary Catherine jabbered hers, and Connor added, "God bless Grandma Gracie." I said a hearty "Amen!" Tucking the covers under their chins, I kissed my grandchicks goodnight and cherished the moments of nesting together.

When Matt and Rebecca returned home, I welcomed them enthusiastically: "Thanks for all you do for those wonderful kids! Hey, next time you need help, just call me—the professional Grandma!"

With that, I packed up my vitamins, Ben-Gay ointment, and heating pad. Then I kissed all my grandchicks, waved good-bye and wobbled, confidently, out the door.

Strengthen the hands that are weak and the knees that are feeble, and make straight paths for your feet.
Hebrews 12:12-13 NASB

Grandmothers Then and Now
(Author Unknown)

Chicken Nugget

In the dim and distant past,
When life's tempo wasn't fast
Grandma used to rock and knit,
Crochet, tat and baby-sit.
When the kids were in a jam,
They could always count on Gram.
In an age of gracious living,
Grandma was the gal for giving.

Grandma now is at the gym,
Exercising to keep slim.
She's off touring with the "bunch,"
Taking clients out to lunch.
Driving North to ski or curl,
All her days are in a whirl.
Nothing seems to stop or block her,
Now that Grandma's off her rocker!

CHAPTER 17

A Few Good Hens

by Rebecca Barlow Jordan

I was a city girl, but somewhere between the ages of six and seven I left my heart in the country. For a brief six-month stint, my family moved to the boonies, where I rode the school bus and rose every morning with the chickens. Then we moved back to the city. But many chicks have hatched and gone since then.

Now married for many years my husband Larry and I had moved from Dallas—a place where I felt half-naked without earrings—to the laid-back town of Greenville, Texas. The small town community was, as one might expect, close-knit. God had been faithful to give me precious friends in the past, but the old seminary warning, "Minister's wives shouldn't have close friends," still fueled my timidity as a newcomer.

I had read scratchings about East Texas hospitality—warm, friendly folk, but cautious: "The hens will either tuck you under their wings, or pluck your tail feathers—if you ruffle theirs." And in a generational town where hens, chicks, and grandchicks all share the same coop, you're bound to ruffle someone's feathers. Or so I'd been told. So far, the only people I had met in our new town were warm "tuckers"—not "pluckers."

While Larry moved gracefully into his new role as associate pastor, I often nested in his study, brooding over the church directory until the service started. Then with confidence bolstered, I would step into the hall. To make friends, I knew I must be friendly. A typical conversation went something like this.

"Hi, Mrs. Green."

"Brown."

"Beg your pardon?"

"Brown. The name is Brown."

"Of course. Brown. Yes, how could I forget?" I turned to the next couple and smiled sweetly." And Mr. and Mrs. . . . I'm sorry, I always have trouble pronouncing your last name."

"Jones."

"What's that?"

"Jones. The name is Jones."

"Well, how are you, Mr. and Mrs. Jones? That color is wonderful for you, Mrs. Jones. You should wear that often!"

Then I made a red-faced, hasty retreat to sit down, hoping I hadn't perched on someone's favorite pew. I finally surrendered in frustration and resorted to, "Hey, sweet lady! How are you today?" Somehow those precious people have not written me off as a wet hen—and I feel more at home each day in our church and our new town.

Just before Larry and I moved to Greenville, a new writing friend called ahead to welcome me. I met Becky a couple of years before where I taught some writing workshops at a conference she attended. Would I like to join their hen gathering as soon as I got settled? Would I! I had just said good-bye to my old writer's group. I welcomed the thought of a new one.

But soon after I hung up the phone, the old hen fears returned: Will they like me? Can a city chic make it in a country coop?

I joined their group, and gradually, my walls of timidity tumbled down. Still, self-doubt tried to strut around— especially during vulnerable moments.

I recently had one of those times nobody likes to crow about. First of all, I felt I had laid a real egg in the class I taught. Thoughts flew out as soon as they entered my brain. I even stuttered a time or two. *I've been teaching for more than 25 years. What's the big deal here?* I wondered.

I dismissed class later than usual and almost knocked down the Chairman of Deacons as I ducked down the back stairs to the choir room. I threw on my robe just as the choir entered the loft and plopped down exhausted while everyone else stood for the call to worship. I'm sure the noise from my throat probably sounded more like croaks or warbles than bona fide notes, but I plastered my face with a smile and sang on anyway.

Later as I pulled into the driveway of our home, I was still feeling flustered, tired from greeting and running, smiling and singing, teaching, and hugging—in desperate need of a word of encouragement—when I noticed something different about my house. A strange object was hanging from my wreath on the front door. Something dead? A harassment? Had I ruffled someone's feathers?

I moved cautiously toward the front door, gripping my keys as a ready weapon. It's an animal—a dead, "yucky" animal hanging from my door! Wait a minute. It's a, It's a . . . *chicken*!

Someone had hung a scraggly, yellow rubber chicken on my front door. As I approached it, I fell to my knees—and let out a series of belly laughs. A fox had crept into my henhouse, and I knew exactly who it was. Gracie! It was Gracie! She had promised to bring some paper so I could finish pecking out the book proposal for our "Hens with Pens" writing group. There beneath the chicken, she had propped the package of paper. I retrieved the ugly thing and called Gracie immediately, leaving a message on her answering machine.

"Gracie! There's no fat, yellow chicken here. But there is one skinny yellow one. And if you're the one who did it, you know what I mean. You gave this chick one much needed cluckle!" Click.

I'm sure Gracie had no idea how long it had been since I had laughed that hard. Her deed was more than nutty. It was— medicine.

Later she called back just as I had drifted off to sleep. "Glad I gave you a laugh," she cackled. "Pass it on to the other hens." And I will—and I did. Like the little man who followed people through squeaky doors with his can of oil, squirting the hinges with a touch of joy to make life more bearable, my new hen friend had reminded me that life is much easier—and better— when we laugh together.

Several months later after the rubber chicken had made its rounds, all five of us writer-hens were eating lunch together at our favorite hangout, Mary of Puddin' Hill. The others had already seated themselves. As I picked up my lunch tray, there on my glass of water hung—you guessed it—a miniature skinny, yellow rubber chicken. I rounded the corner and headed toward our table. Silence. Our eyes met, and then hen grins popped out, and the cackling began all over again. My initiation complete, I knew I was "in" with the hens.

It feels good to finally find a place to roost again. I think maybe I'm going to really like it here.

> *Two are better than one . . . If one falls down,*
> *his friend can help him up. But pity the [one] who falls*
> *and has no one to help him up!*
> Ecclesiastes 4:9-10

God Made Friends

© 1998, Kristonne Corp. Used by Permission.

Chicken Nugget

God knew our lives would be richer
with the addition of a special relationship—
Someone who would tend our hearts and
mend our dreams—
Someone who would give without asking
in return—
Someone who would love without judgment,
and believe, regardless of the circumstances.
God did not create us to laugh or cry alone—
That's why He made friends.

Section III

Under His Wings

Confidence in God's Love

CHAPTER 18

The Red Hen Rides Again (*And* Again)

by Fran Caffey Sandin

What appeared to be a *simple* sport, turned into an ordeal that would ruffle the feathers of any middle-aged hen.

It all began when my husband Jim decided to introduce our family to the joys of snow skiing. Our teenage son and daughter immediately donned boots, skis, and poles. After a couple of practice runs, they zoomed off for higher ground, leaving us in a cloud of powder. Where? On the bunny slope.

Feeling like the famous red hen in my scarlet ski jacket, I sat beside Jim in the lift chair and, as we ascended, thought, *How romantic. Here we are on this beautiful snow-covered slope and the instructions sound so easy, too.* The guide said, "All you have to do is lean forward and ski away."

I glanced at my husband and he smiled—seeming confident, calm, and relaxed. But I barely had time to adjust goggles, wipe my nose, and check my gloves before looking up and seeing the sign. "Jim!" I nervously gasped, "It says *Unload Here!*"

Jim leaned forward and skied off to one side. *But I'm not ready yet,* I thought. *I need a little more time to think about this.* My pounding heart was saying, *Stop-STOP, Stop, STOP!* but the monster chair kept right on moving. When I tried to stand up, my backside froze to the seat. Finally, gathering all my courage, I grabbed the metal arm, gave a big heave-ho and lunged forward. After a brief zip on the skis, I landed on my bottom and slid into a heap. It was astonishing to me how quickly a ski lift can turn into a snow drift. Two ski patrol guys smoothly zigzagged out of their small cedar house.

"Are you OK?" they asked while hoisting me out of the way of oncoming skiers.

"Oh, yes, I'm fine, just fine. Thanks so much!" I repeated profusely.

Determined, I stood up, brushed off the snow, straightened my hat, and pointed my skis downhill. At first I moved slowly. Then I began picking up speed. About halfway down I lost all semblance of control. Whizzing past other skiers, the only emergency measure I could think of was to scream, "Watch out! Here I come!"

Finally, in the midst of my panic, a rational thought broke through. I remembered the instructor's warning, "To slow down, make a wedge." So I pushed my heels outward and tucked my toes inward. This creative move succeeded in locking the front of my skis together, at which point I fell like a domino face-first into the thick, fluffy snow. As several experts swished by my crumpled form, I suddenly felt "on stage" and wondered, *Why, oh why, did I wear this bright red jacket? If only I'd chosen a white or even a pine green ski suit—perhaps no one would have noticed.* As it was, I might as well have been flashing a neon sign that said, "Look over here! See the clumsiest woman on earth!"

Somehow I survived one descent, and then, in spite of my dwindling confidence, I went back to the bunny lift. I was so anxious about departing the lift, I fell off again. And again. And again. And again, until I decided it would be better for my sagging psyche if I just stopped keeping count. Once, as we neared the patrol house, I heard the guides moan, "Oh no, here she comes again!" Poor fellas. I'm sure they were nursing hernias from repeatedly hauling me away.

Nearing the end of the day, I stopped and gave myself a little lecture. *Look, Fran, you have to learn how to get off this lift or you'll never see the mountaintop.* Remembering *The Little Engine That Could*, I began telling myself, *I think I can, I think I can.* Then a tip from a stranger changed my day.

After my last splat, another woman near my vintage skied over to me, bent down, and whispered, "Honey—If you'll scoot your bottom up to the edge of the chair *before* you unload, it'll be easier to stay up." Oh. Why hadn't I thought of that before?

To my utter amazement and delight—it worked! The next opportunity, I inched toward the front of the seat. At just the right time, I managed to get up and, while wobbling in all directions, skied away *on my own.* The guides began shouting, "Yeah, she made it!"—and everyone else joined in—including me—"Yeah, I made it!"

My ecstasy was short-lived. The next morning, I felt like a rubber chicken that had been used as a baseball bat. Every muscle in my body ached. I found some muscles I didn't even know I had! As I gingerly strained my way up the slope, I kept my eyes on the mountaintop and thought, *Somehow, I'm going to get up there.*

The first order of the day was to take another ski lesson. A group of us waited until Rusty, the chief instructor, put us to a test. He glided to the bottom of the hill and asked each one to ski down so he could evaluate our form and assign us to the appropriate class.

I watched the others; most were poised and controlled. Then came my turn.

I began cautiously, but quickly approached Olympic speed. Instead of remembering "the wedge" that might have averted my Kamikaze run, I barely missed Rusty by veering off to one side where I maneuvered 180 degrees and crash-landed into the orange net fence. It was *so—so unladylike*. At least I made the instructor's job easy. He assigned everyone else to an intermediate class, then as if I were a small child, he held out his hand and said, "Come with me."

After Rusty had helped me to my feet, he flashed a good-natured grin and observed, "I see you need a little help with your parallel turns." No kidding. At first, I wanted to melt into the snow and disappear, but by the time Rusty spent a few hours instructing and encouraging me, my outlook had changed. *I'm so glad I hit that fence*, I thought as I shwish-shwished my way down the hill. *God has turned my disaster into a blessing! Look at all the individual attention I'm getting!*

On the third day, Jim and I took the lift to the top! What a spectacular view. The hush of fresh powder, punctuated by the aroma of evergreens, lent an awesome air to the blanketed valley below. I felt like singing "How Great Thou Art" closely followed by "The Hallelujah Chorus"—to celebrate my victory.

Life, in many ways, reminds me of skiing. We have lots of ups and downs, numerous lumps and bumps. But if we keep our eyes on the Maker of Mountains, He'll pick us up when we fall, and sometimes He'll even carry us. Like Rusty, God knows when we need personal attention. Like Jim, He is patient and kind. And even when it feels like a sky full of snow is falling on our heads, and we feel we can't make it to the top, it's reassuring to know *He thinks I can, He thinks I can.*

The steps of a man are established by the LORD;
And He delights in his way.
When he falls, he shall not be hurled headlong;
Because the LORD is the One who holds his hand.
Psalm 37:23-24 NASB

Texas Chili
(to warm your chicken heart)

Chicken Nugget

1. Brown 1-2 lbs. boneless chicken breasts in a large pot with 1 clove garlic, 1 tsp. chili powder, and 1 tsp. cumin. Set aside, cool, cut into cubes. (May use prepared chicken tenders instead.) Place in bowl.

2. In the same large pot, sauté in 2 Tbsp. oil, 2 medium onions, 2 green peppers, 2 chopped carrots, 1 8-oz. package of fresh mushrooms, 1 clove garlic, 2 tsp. chili powder, 2 tsp. cumin.

3. To large pot, add chicken, 1 28-oz. can tomatoes, 1 28-oz. can tomato puree, 1 can kidney beans, 1 can black beans, 1-2 chopped jalapeno peppers, 2 Tbsp. brown sugar, 2 tsp. chili powder, 1 tsp. cummin, 1/2 tsp. pepper, 1 tsp. salt. Simmer for 3 hours.

CHAPTER 19

Covered by His Feathers

by Rebecca Barlow Jordan

"Vacation—Yes!" The very mention of the word brought visions of quiet, hassle-free, getaway places for Mom and Dad, along with fun-filled adventures for the kids. However, somehow "hassle-free" never quite seemed to materialize for us. No matter how carefully we planned—something always went awry. Overheated cars and overtired bodies usually spelled overtaxed emotions. However, every year bravely we loaded up "Old Yeller," our faithful car, and headed out again, confident this vacation would be different.

And one year it was. Different. But not in the way we'd expected.

We were Colorado-bound—to our favorite vacation spot. Only a few miles from home, I inhaled deeply. "I can almost smell it now—crisp mountain air, fragrant pines—"

"Mom, she's on my side of the car. Make her move over!" My daughters' voices interrupted my reverie.

"Hey!" I chirped, trying to divert their attention. "Who wants to read our vacation Psalm this time?" The reading of Psalm 91 was a family tradition on our trips. Many times its words comforted us, preparing us for unknown vacation pitfalls. (As a mother, I often wondered if the "pestilence that stalks in the darkness, and the plague that destroys at midday" meant fighting children and self-destructive cars on vacation.) Glares and stares from the back seat said—*you* read it. So I did, and the atmosphere relaxed.

We had planned to spend that summer night in Farmington, New Mexico, but decided instead to travel on to Durango, Colorado. Unknowingly we took a wrong turn. Little did any of us know where one wrong turn would take us—and that it would actually prove to be a God-detour.

About noon, our ten-year-old Chevy began to lose power, and sounds of serious chug-a-chugging poured from under the hood. "Old Yeller" heaved a huge sigh and expired. Larry carefully steered her off the main highway. He checked Old Yeller's yawning metal mouth for engine problems, while we huddled inside her upholstered abdomen. When he returned, the news confirmed our worst suspicions: The plague that destroys at midday has hit. No vacation this summer.

Larry prayed, assuring the girls we had committed the vacation to God. He could certainly be trusted to handle this small detour. *Detour or dead end?* I mused under my breath. We gave thanks for whatever was about to happen, even if it meant returning home early. "Send us some help, Lord," Larry prayed. *Please!* I added a silent P.S.

Larry managed to start the car again and inched it back slowly toward a gas station two or three hundred yards away— then the car died. The gas station stood empty. The awning flapped noisily in the wind, mocking us like some mirage in the desert. Across the highway, however, Larry noticed a faded sign in the midst of several small trailers: "Midway Body Shop." *Midway to where?* I wondered. He walked up to the main trailer and knocked on the door.

A short, stocky woman opened it and eyed Larry suspiciously. "Who are you, and what do you want?" After much hesitation and a glance at his pastor's business card, she finally agreed to let him use the phone. Larry's attempts to find help soon failed. At that point, the woman called her son-in-law, Juan, a mechanic in the body shop behind her home. We nursed our car across the highway into the dirt driveway, where Juan met us and expertly lifted the hood.

He smiled. "Only a broken rocker arm."

Of all the major things that could go wrong with a car that had racked up 95,000 miles, a broken rocker indeed sounded benign. Actually, I didn't know the difference between a rocker arm and a swaying leg. But Juan's cheerful, positive attitude convinced me the problem was not too serious. He pawed through the greasy car parts of the body shop. There, in one corner of the room, lay an engine like Old Yeller's with a working rocker arm and an accompanying "push rod"— whatever that was. (It made Juan grin, so I smiled too.)

However, we weren't out of the garage yet. Juan gravely informed us he still needed something called a "valve cover gasket," so he and Larry headed seven miles into Farmington in search of the precious part. As I watched them chug away in Juan's faded green pickup, I noticed the truck had no hood to cover its sputtering engine. *Looks like Juan's been through a "plague" or two,* I mused.

As they drove around town, Larry discovered a hidden layer beneath Juan's apparent cheerfulness. Circumstances in his past had embittered Juan and almost shattered the remaining shreds of his faith. The cheerful smile was merely a protective covering, a self-defensive shield to shut out the invisible hurt. But, like his hoodless jalopy, Juan exposed the inner workings of his heart to Larry. While Larry and Juan were gone, Juan's wife and mother took me and our daughters into their home, fed us, and fussed over us like a pair of mother hens. Together, we shared precious moments celebrating stories of God's goodness in our lives.

Two hours later, the men returned. Every auto parts store had closed down for the evening.

"Not to worry," said Juan, still smiling.

As an afterthought, Juan checked another corner of the body shop for the needed part. There, on the wall, he discovered two brand new valve cover gaskets that fit our car perfectly.

Juan—that sweet, good Samaritan—worked nonstop without supper, despite our urging him to take a break. From five o'clock in the afternoon until eleven-thirty that night, Juan hovered over our car, meticulously repairing the damage. When the last part was securely in place, Juan closed the hood of the car and grinned. Grease blotched his hands, his face, and his clothes. But in the dim light of that garage, when Juan turned around, we half-expected to see him sprout wings and a golden halo appear above his grimy sport cap.

Our family joined hands in a circle with Juan, his expectant wife, and their three children. We offered thanks for the miracle of a repaired vehicle, a salvaged vacation—and the new friends God had given us. As we started to climb back in "Old Yeller," Larry reached for his wallet. The young man shook his head no.

"You'll rob me of a blessing if you don't let me pay you," my husband insisted.

"No, you'll steal one from me if you do," said Juan earnestly, tears rolling down his cheeks.

I'm sure Juan believed Larry was heaven-sent that day to encourage him and spark his faith in God once again. But to us, Juan had seemed the blessing—plopped down in the middle of nowhere—sent to prove God's caring and provision were equal to every crisis. We hugged Juan and his family and left rejoicing—half crying, half laughing with thanks to God for His faithfulness.

About midnight that night, we settled into a Farmington motel back on the right road, exhausted from our ordeal. I pulled the covers close to my face that night. They felt feathery soft and strangely comforting—sort of like God's protective wings.

I was almost asleep when I heard a familiar whine: "Mom, she's on my side of the bed. Make her move over!" I closed my eyes and rolled over with a fake snore, quoting silently, *You will not fear . . . the pestilence that stalks in the darkness.*

He will cover you with his feathers,
and under his wings you will find refuge;
his faithfulness will be your shield and rampart.
Psalm 91:4

Chicken Nugget

Rebecca's Quick Chick Goodies
for Mini-meals on Wheels
"Cinnamon Snicker Chicks"

1 Box White Cake Mix
½ Cup Vegetable Oil
2 Eggs (Can use egg substitute)
1 tsp. Cinnamon

Preheat oven to 350 degrees. Mix ingredients well
with spoon. Place by teaspoonfuls, one inch apart on
ungreased cookie sheet. If desired, press down
gently to form round-shaped cookies. Bake 6 to 9
minutes, or just before edges brown. Cookies baked
less will appear doughy, but will be chewier; longer
baking time will make crisp chicken feed! For
variety, add raisins or nuts to form eyes and beaks.
Form large round cookies for big chicks. Remove
from pan and place on paper towels to cool. The
chicks will love 'em—hens and roosters, too!

CHAPTER 20

The Sky Is Falling

by Susan Duke

They were the words every mother prays she will not hear. Words I had told God I could never bear.

"I'm so sorry," the doctor spoke almost in a whisper, "we couldn't save your son Thomas."

"You must be mistaken . . . this can't be true. You must have my son confused with someone else."

I grabbed the doctor's hands and searched his eyes for any fragment of hope. But as he gently shook his head, the sorrow expressed in his tear-filled eyes told me there was nothing left to say. From a place deeper than I ever knew existed within my soul, a slow wailing groan permeated all of my senses and took me to my knees.

How could this be? God knew I could not bear this.

Leaving the hospital that cold October night, I spoke six words to a friend who drove me home: "I'll never be the same again."

I wasn't even fully conscious of what I had said, for I was focused on the grim task at hand—of going home to wait for my husband, on his way home from a business trip, unaware of what he would be facing when he walked in the door. My daughter, who lived two hours away, was also en route, not knowing that her brother was gone. I had called her husband at work and told him all I knew at the time: that Thomas had been involved in a serious automobile accident and they needed to come.

As friends received word of the shocking news, they quickly poured into our home. Even with all the people around, I never felt more alone as I retreated to my bedroom and closed the door. The sky had fallen and there was no comfort to be found. I sat in darkness, waiting for my family to arrive. My heart was more than shattered; it felt as if it had been permanently removed. I was numb, and void of any feeling, other than emptiness. How could my son—so energetic and dynamic, so happy and full of dreams—not be coming home? I had hugged him good-bye only this morning before he went to see a friend. *Lord, he's only 18!*

The first months after Thomas's death, grief knocked at our heart's door three more times. It was as if we were in the midst of a never-ending storm of sorrow. Just two weeks after my son's funeral, a dear friend who was like a brother to us died suddenly of an aneurysm. Then my best friend Nell, who had been battling cancer for six months, died just days before Christmas. Finally, in January, the sudden death of my 21-year-old nephew Marty, sent us reeling once again. My sister Pat had already lost one son. She had come to be at our side in October, and now she was facing a terrible loss again. Would this hurricane of grief ever end?

All of us think tragedy is something that happens to others, until we are suddenly the ones feeling as though we're trapped in someone else's nightmare. I plan to write a book sometime in the near future about all the things I have learned and continue to learn about grief, because books penned by others who had suffered a loss were so instrumental in my start toward recovery from grief. Each volume I purchased or received as a gift became like a cherished friend of solace.

I learned as I read that everyone grieves differently. I had a year's worth of speaking engagements scheduled before Thomas' accident. I chose not to cancel them. Staying busy and speaking out about my grief brought a measure of healing. But whenever I came back and retreated to the comfort of my own home, I found I had an overwhelming need to just be alone, to grieve deeply and privately. It was then that torrents of tears flowed freely, forever marking the pages in the journals written by other kindred spirit sufferers, whose pilgrimage I was now sharing. I vowed that someday with God's help I, too, would reach out and minister words of comfort and understanding to others.

It has been 7 years since that long ride home from the hospital when I spoke the words, "I'll never be the same again." I now realize that I never spoke truer words. My life and the life of my family were changed forever that fateful October afternoon. But, what amazed me then—and continues to amaze me now—is the power of God's love and grace through it all.

In those early months of grief, we literally felt God's grace as an almost physical embrace—as though a cocoon had been wrapped around us, carrying us, protecting us, even warming us. Those who have experienced this envelopment of grace understand what I am struggling to put in human terms. I had never realized how intimate God's grace could be, I guess because we had never needed it as badly as we needed it in this crisis. The storm weathered on, but it was as if we were given raincoats of love, invisible armor, to protect us from the sky falling down on our hearts.

When an acorn fell on Chicken Little's head, in the classic children's story, she feared the acorn was a piece of the sky and went running for cover, crying, "The sky is falling! The sky is falling!" She thought the best way to handle her fear was to run from it, avoid it, and seek protection. We all have some Chicken Little in us.

There were times when I, too, felt like Chicken Little—longing for a cave where I could hide away. When the sky really does fall in our lives, so often we think that in order to cope and protect ourselves from further pain, we must shut ourselves away, only occasionally peeping out at life from the safety of our dark shelter. We withdraw and don't trust anything outside of our cave.

I have seen many people so devastated by grief that their lives become nothing but bitter shrines to their losses. Of all things, it was in reading the historical account of the despair of the pilgrims who came to America that I gained a valuable insight about loss.

Though the pilgrims lost more than half of their own number, they made a conscious choice as they carried their precious ones to a field for burial. They did not mark their graves with even one small stone—so the Indians would not know the extent of their losses. Instead, they planted their burial field with corn.

Of course, I'm not suggesting that we don't mark and treasure our loved one's grave. But we all have to choose whether or not we are going to build a monument over our grief, making ourselves a vulnerable target for evil forces of bitterness and hate. Or we can choose to plant a field of harvest in the soil of our loss.

Today, as I type these words from my heart, it is strangely warmed, for I work on my words in what once was the room of my precious son. Now it is a writing study, my field of harvest.

Someone once said, "False hope expects to find relief from suffering. True hope finds God in suffering." Courage is not the absence of fear and despair, but the capacity to move forward, confidently trusting the Maker of the heavens to cover us with the shadow of His mighty hand, even if the sky should fall.

> *I have put my words in your mouth*
> *and covered you with the shadow of my hand—*
> *I who set the heavens in place,*
> *who laid the foundations of the earth . . .*
> *Sorrow and sighing will flee away.*
> *I, even I, am He who comforts you.*
> Isaiah 51:16

Chicken Nugget

Have Courage
Victor Hugo

Have courage for the great sorrows of life and patience for the small ones; and when you have laboriously accomplished your daily task, go to sleep in peace. God is awake.

CHAPTER 21

The Egg-citement of Creativity

by Becky Freeman

I call him the Renaissance Man. My friend, Reg Grant, is creativity on the loose. An Emmy Award-winning actor for his starring role in films, he writes scripts, books, plays; creates and performs dozens of voices for an innovative children's radio show; and in his spare time teaches seminary students how not to bore their congregations.

Ideas pop out of Reg's head like pastries from a toaster. He's enthusiasm personified. When Reg invited me over to discuss a project (or two, or twenty) I could hardly wait to see his home. Walking up to his front door, I couldn't help but imagine the theme song from *Leave it to Beaver* playing in the background—his 2-story house is a near replica of June and Ward Cleaver's, nestled in a tree-lined, all-American neighborhood. However, Reg is such a kid at heart, he's much more like Beav than the sensible Ward.

When Reg showed me the family backyard with two— count 'em *two*—tree houses, his exact words were, "Here's where we play!" Between explaining the ins and outs of complicated new projects, Reg punctuated his sentences with sudden bursts of gratitude. "Isn't this fun? Can you believe this exciting stuff?" He was enthralled with everything from his son's stuffed animals (inspiration for his children's radio show), to his teenage girl's "creativity wall," to a hot-off-the press computer program, to music pouring from his homemade entertainment room, to miscellaneous thoughts about God's creative ways. To be with Reg is to experience coming at the world as a child again—open armed and wide-eyed.

When I needed some information on a children's project, Reg suggested I telephone a friend of his, Bob Singleton. Bob writes much of the creative Barney the Dinosaur music that kids love. (And parents tolerate.)

When Bob's secretary answered the phone, she literally sang her hello making a tune out of, "Hello, Beck-y, we've been ex-pect-ing your call!" When Bob answered the phone, I explained I was a friend of Reg's, then added, "I'm calling to say I think two of you are having entirely too much fun to call it 'work.'"

"Yeah," Bob answered and by the sound of his voice, I could only assume he was playing with a yo-yo in the background. "We're just a couple of creative A-D-D kids who can't get a real job."

So maybe that's it, I thought as I pondered those words later in the evening. *I've never been able to keep a real job either. Perhaps I'm not crazy after all—maybe I'm just really creative.*

What makes a person creative? Climbing tree houses? Eccentricity? Neglecting the mundane for loftier pursuits? (Sure, Einstein discovered relativity—but did he ever figure out how to use a comb?) If forgetfulness turns out to be indicative of a creative streak, I'm a shoe in.

Today I accidentally drove past my destination point, the mall, no less than three times. My thirteen-year-old daughter was nearly beside herself with frustration. "Moooother! You're just like that dorky Anne of Green Gables we're reading about in English. Stop thinking all those fancy thoughts and talking about the meaning of life and *drive.*" Oh, the burden of being a creative soul.

Recently I stopped by a hen friend's homey coop for a visit.

"What's up, Beck?" Suzie asked as she led me to the cozy breakfast nook in her rustic log cabin. I watched as she poured French vanilla creamer into two mugs of hot coffee.

"Well . . . let's see . . . " I answered, as I reached gratefully for a steaming mug. "First of all, as you know, I'm up to my feathers in this chicken epic the five of us are pecking out together." I paused to take a sip as Suzie settled in the chair across from me.

"Then," I continued, "I'm traveling and speaking some, doing lots of radio interviews, and working on a couple of new book proposals. I'm also finishing up a short-term career as a literary agent. It was so fulfilling, helping new writers get book contracts, but there are other things I want to pursue now— some childrens' books, and a book about simplifying life."

"Back up, Becky. Did you say a book about simplifying life?"

"Yes, well, actually it's about my complicated search for simplicity. Oh, Suzie—you know what I'd love to do next?"

"You mean that you aren't already doing?"

"Yes! I'd love to learn to paint. On one of those old-time easels. Outside. In a meadow. In the spring. And clogging—I'd like to get a pair of those lace-up boots and learn to clog up a storm to . . . 'The Orange Blossom Special' . . . And—"

"Becky," Suzie interrupted, "I don't mean to squelch your spirit or anything, but aren't you carrying this creativity thing a little too far?"

"Okay. Yes. But I think I'm doing okay—I mean, I still comb my hair and all. It's just that I see other people doing all these fascinating things, and I end up wanting a taste of what they're having."

"But how are you going to keep up this schedule?"

"I don't know. The other night Scott suggested I start writing 'sleep' on my 'to-do' list."

Suzie leaned her head on her hand and moaned softly. "Just listening to you makes my head spin. . . ."

"I know. I should make it a policy never to say all I'm involved in out loud. It scares people. But the thing is, I *love* what I'm doing. I know I can't do it all and I really do have to cut back, but I wake up in the morning and there's this—this zing in my heart."

"Zing?"

"Zing. There's no other word for it. People used to tease me about being dingy. Now I guess I'm zingy dingy."

Creativity so fascinates me that—no joke—I am currently reading, simultaneously, six books on the subject.

While I was doing some Anne of Green Gables-style pondering on the topic of creativity, I thought about the Source of all creativity. In the book of Genesis I saw that God enjoyed creating the universe. And He paused now and again, after each phase of creation, to comment on how good it was.

As I was rereading the familiar story of Adam in the Garden of Eden, it also occurred to me for the first time ever, that God very deliberately involved Adam in the creative process. When the time came to create Eve, God could have just—Zap!— plunked her down right there next to Adam. But He didn't. Instead, He took the long way around.

He began by asking Adam to give names to the animals. Then like a proud parent, God simply watched to see what Adam would call them. Whatever Adam named the animals, that's the name that would stick. He gave Adam lots of creative space—no heavy manuals, or "Naming the Animals Guidelines." Basically, it was your simple "name 'em and claim 'em" operation.

Eventually, Adam realized that all these animals had partners—but that he, the man of the garden, had come up short one mate. It was an "Ah-hah!" moment. God had brought Adam to what psychologists call "a point of felt need." Then God caused Adam to fall asleep, took a rib from his side, and fashioned a woman. Examine this again in slow motion: God took a part of Adam, mixed it creatively with His Spirit and—voila!—a whole new creation. God purposely involved and included Adam in the creative process. Why?

Perhaps He knew that Adam would cherish what he had some part in creating. After all, when Adam woke up, almost the first words out of his mouth were, "She is bone of my bone! Flesh of my flesh!" He was thrilled to have shared in Eve's creation. Don't you love the ingenuity of God? How He prefers working with us, and through us, so we too can experience the zing of creativity? Or as Renaissance Reg puts it—"Isn't this fun? Can you believe this exciting stuff?" Kind of makes you want to go paint the ceiling of a cathedral, or compose an oratorio with a full orchestra in response to such love.

Or, at the very least, it makes me want to put on a pair of clogging shoes and do a little foot-stomping jig.

In the beginning God created.
Genesis 1:1 KJV

Chicken Nugget

Secrets from Famous Creative Eggs-amples

Steamboat Writer
"The man with a new idea is a crank until the idea succeeds."

Mark Twain

Computer Game Guy
"Nolan Bushnell, the founder of the Atari Company, got the inspiration for what became a best-selling video game while idly flicking sand on a beach."

The Creative Spirit by Daniel Goleman,
Paul Kaufman, Michael Ray

Genius with Bad Hair
Albert Einstein's fascination with physics began when he was just five, when he was ill in bed. His father brought him a present—a small magnetic compass. For hours Einstein lay in bed, entranced by the needle that infallibly pointed the way north. When he was close to seventy, Einstein said, "This experience made a deep and lasting impression on me. Something deeply hidden had to be behind things."

The Creative Spirit by Daniel Goleman,
Paul Kaufman, Michael Ray

CHAPTER 22

When My Wings Were Clipped

by Gracie Malone

There are a lot of things in life we all take for granted and, until you lose it, health is probably one of them.

For instance, most of us pay little attention to our skin unless it needs lotion or a dab of moisturizer. As long as it does its job and doesn't cause problems, we don't even think about it. Our brains are cluttered with other data. Kids, on the other hand, with their fresh, inquisitive minds ponder everything. And sometimes they reach mind-boggling conclusions.

One evening when our grandson Connor was four, he stepped from the bathtub and backed into the fluffy towel I held up for him. Then he shivered and said, "Grandma Gracie, I'm cold!" I rubbed his arms and legs briskly to make the goosebumps go away, then circled him with my arms.

Connor grinned as he said, "I'd really be cold if I didn't have skin."

Long after Connor was sleeping soundly, I was puzzling over what he'd said. I guess a kid without skin would be cold, like a chicken without feathers, or a cat without fur. But

Connor's words brought a deeper message to me. God was reminding me, be thankful for the familiar, that which we take for granted—like your skin.

I smiled, recalling the time when my skin was literally coming apart.

It all began the morning I noticed a peculiar blister erupting on my chest. Within a week it was followed by a rash of watery eruptions, then black, crusty sores. Eventually a huge area of open flesh covered my chest. After six weeks of tedious medical examinations, a biopsy, and several unsuccessful treatments, we finally found a doctor who knew what was wrong.

"I think you have the same illness as the patriarch Job," he said. "It is a rare auto-immune disease. Instead of adhering, your skin cells are reacting against each other. We must treat this condition with chemotherapy drugs and steroids."

I reacted by asking two questions foremost in every sick chick's head: "How long will this take?" and "Will I lose my hair?"

As the doctor wrote out prescriptions and gave instructions for my care, he said, "Gracie, I believe you will recover, but you have to be patient. Perhaps by the end of the year there will be an improvement." It was August 1.

That evening Joe and I gathered our brood for a family conference. Our sons reacted with compassion. One major concern was how their mom, the woman who lives life "in the vaseline" (as my son had interpreted "fast lane" when he was a child) would handle being confined to the home coop for five months. Little did we know that the five anticipated months were an underestimate. It would be spring before I was well again.

Every morning I went through a painful ritual of cleansing my skin, applying sterile compresses, swirling on protective cream, and carefully measuring out increasing doses of medicine. After taking the medicine, I rested in bed, avoiding even the slightest movement that would cause more pain. By afternoon the excruciating effects of the medicine subsided and I could read, watch TV, or talk with eight-year-old Jason. After dinner Joe would help me back to bed. The nights were long, often punctuated with bad dreams.

The medicine also caused some frightening side effects. One morning I caught a glimpse of myself in the mirror; I was one odd-looking bird. Lifeless tufts of hair jutted out in all directions from an almost bald head. My face was moon-shaped from steroids, my eyes sunken, my complexion a sallow gray. In addition, the large doses of cortisone produced cataracts that clouded my vision. I burst out crying.

Though by nature I am not prone to moodiness, I was beyond feeling blue: I was depressed. I had dedicated my life to God and thought we were friends, but when I needed Him most, I felt forgotten and alone. This dreaded feeling was worse than any physical pain! "God, why did this happen?" I asked. "Have I sinned? Are You punishing me? Do You love me?"

The next morning I propped myself up in bed with a mound of pillows, opened my Bible, and with my magnifying glass read the words, "I have loved you with an everlasting love" (Jeremiah 31:3).

Today I marvel that I, a frail chicken with a pea-sized brain, had the audacity to challenge the Almighty. But I'll never forget my reaction to reading that verse. "No, You don't!" I yelled. In a fit of frustration, I grasped a handful of pages and tried to rip them out, but they were sewn in too tightly and I was too weak. I slammed the Bible on the nightstand and sobbed.

That evening I had to tell my husband the latest development. "Joe, I'm going blind. I couldn't read today without the magnifying glass." Joe knelt beside my bed and prayed, "Lord, please don't let her lose her sight. Please make Gracie well again."

Gradually my condition improved. New skin cells reproduced, covering exposed nerve endings and providing a healthy barrier against life-threatening germs. I gained strength, the depression lifted, and my attitude changed. The cataracts cleared, and I could focus and read my Bible again.

As soon as I could make out words on a page, I turned in the *Old Testament* and located the book of Job. As I read, I felt a special kinship with him. I discovered that Job argued with God, too. "What charges do You have against me? Does it please You to oppress me?" (Job 10:2-3). Later, I was blessed by Job's faith: "Though he slay me, yet will I hope in him" (Job 13:15). I realized that God loved Job and was not punishing him. God said, "There is no one on earth like him; he is blameless and upright, a man who fears God and shuns evil" (Job 1:8).

As I pondered these verses, a spiritual healing was taking place deep beneath my skin—in my heart. As I learned to live by faith instead of by my feelings, I found rest in the shadow of God's wings.

Family members and friends became God's representatives. Our pastor provided encouragement, prayer, and books. Church members called or sent cards to cheer me. Friends took turns driving me to the doctor's office. Others helped with household chores, picked up prescriptions, and brought food.

One day Jason asked, "Mom, what are we having for supper?"

"Oh, Honey, I don't know. But you know what I wish?" Jason shook his head, then I finished my thought. "I wish I were well enough to cook a hot, steaming bowlful of chicken and dumplings for you."

"And chocolate pie!" Jason added.

"Yeah!" I agreed, smacking my lips—"and chocolate pie. As soon as I'm well, Jason, as soon as I'm well."

A few hours later the doorbell rang. Unaware of our conversation, one of my friends stood at the door bearing a gift in a big steaming pot: chicken and dumplings! Before Joe could set the table, another friend arrived with dessert. Yes, a chocolate pie.

As I took a bite of the warm dumplings, sampled the pie and sipped coffee, I thought, "You do, don't You? You do love me with everlasting love."

Even in the midst of pain and sorrow, He is there. He knows. He cares.

Never will I leave you; never will I forsake you.
Hebrews 13:5

Chicken Nugget

Things to Do as You Recooperate

1. Put all your loose photos into albums.
2. Create individual albums as a special gift for each child.
3. Keep a journal. Record blessings and answers to prayer.
4. Collect get well cards and notes in a pretty basket. Read them whenever you feel lonely or depressed.
5. Spray the sheets and pillow cases with your favorite perfume.
6. Read the books you always wanted to read but didn't have time to.
7. Attempt small projects like cleaning out nightstand drawers.
8. Write letters and thank-you notes. Call your friends.

CHAPTER 23

All God's Brood

by Susan Duke

Betty Pickitt and her husband (whom I always just called "Pickitt") lived two houses down from us when I was a child growing up in East Texas. I remember going to their house every day, on my own, just to say hello or to see what Betty might be cooking on her old wood stove. Everything smelled so good at Betty and Pickitt's. Especially, I remember the sweet potatoes. It seemed like every time I went for a visit, those sweet potatoes would be baking and almost ready to eat. Betty would always say, "Sugar, you're just in time for some mighty good vittles." The fact that Betty and Pickitt were Black and I was not never entered my little 4-year-old mind. All I knew was that they were my friends, and I loved them like most kids love a grandmother and granddaddy. I felt safe and always welcome in their home.

Looking back, I remember how Betty and Pickitt always seemed to be amused by our conversations. They were genuinely interested in my childlike view of life. Sometimes they would read me a story from the well-worn Bible that often lay open on the kitchen table. They took time to answer my questions, and I remember having the sense that they always wished I would stay just a little longer. Many times Betty would send me home with a few still-warm baked sweet potatoes tucked under my small arms. She'd say, "Now you run on home and take these to your mama." I felt so grownup and proud when I handed Mama those sweet potatoes.

One day when I arrived home, Mama got a dish towel and wiped fresh sweet potato from the corners of my mouth. Then she asked, "Why is it that you won't ever eat sweet potatoes when I cook them?"

I explained simply, "They just taste better at Betty's house."

Maybe it was the old wood stove she cooked them in, or perhaps it was the way she heaped on fresh butter and a pinch of salt. Whatever the reason, I can remember their unique taste and, to this day, another sweet potato has never matched that taste. Even more, I can picture Betty's smiling face as she handed me a plate and then winked at Pickitt, watching me intently as I devoured the much-appreciated feast. I don't recall a single visit that Betty didn't have something cooked and ready to serve. Giving was a way of life to them.

Some days, Pickitt would stop by our house on his way into town. When Mama answered the door, Pickitt would tip his hat and ask, "Ma'am, is there anything I can bring you from town?"

"No, but thanks for asking," Mama would usually say.

"Well, then, ma'am," Pickitt would continue, "Would you mind if I bring back a little somethin' for Miss Suzie?"

"That'll be fine," Mama would reply.

Pickitt would then lean down, smile that big smile of his and say, "And what would Miss Suzie like ol' Pickitt to bring her from town today? Will it be candy corn or cashew nuts?"

Sitting on the front porch steps, eagerly awaiting Pickitt's return, I remember thinking, *If Betty and Pickitt love me this much, I must be someone special.*

With the passage of years, I realize now more than ever that we indeed shared a special friendship, one that defied age and race differences. It was a friendship born of love, acceptance, peace, and joy. It was the kind of friendship that does not recognize prejudice or status in life, but only what my heart knew as real love. When Pickitt handed me my much-anticipated package and I said, "Thank you, Sir," the expression on his face said, *Child, you just made my day!*

Another fond childhood memory I have is of Pickitt and Betty raising turkeys behind their house. The turkeys fascinated me with the funny sounds they made. I told Pickitt one day when he was out feeding them, "It sounds like those turkeys are talkin'."

He responded, "Why sure they are Missy; they're talkin' turkey."

"Well, can you understand what they are sayin'?" I asked.

"Sometimes I can," Pickitt answered.

My curious childhood imagination took over as I continued to probe, "What are they sayin' right now?"

Pickitt knelt down until he was even with me, looked straight into my eyes, wide with wonder, and said, "Why, Miss Suzie, I do believe those turkeys are sayin' how glad they are to see you. That's why they make so much commotion when you come around."

Believing every word he spoke, I waved to the whole lot and exclaimed, "I'm very glad to see you too!"

Pickitt chuckled out loud, patted me on the head and in his friendly way replied, "Oh Miss Suzie, what you just won't do."

A few days later on yet another visit, Pickitt called me over to the turkey pen and pointed to the young turkeys that were roaming about.

"You know, Miss Suzie, Thanksgiving will be coming up in a few months, and I've just been thinkin' that you might like to pick out a turkey of your own for me to raise just for you." I quickly pointed to the best looking of all. Pickitt pulled a colored string out of his overall pocket and handed it to me.

"Well, all right now," he said. "Let's catch him and tie this string on his leg so we'll know for sure which one is Miss Suzie's turkey." I never gave the fate of the doomed bird a thought. I was too caught up in the excitement of Pickitt letting me capture and tag my own Thanksgiving turkey. I felt proud, as if a special honor had been bestowed upon me. Pickitt suggested we name him Tom.

My daily visits found me looking anxiously inside the pen for Tom, the grandest turkey in the place with the red string tied to his leg. Pickitt told Mama about our adventure and said she could be expecting ol' Tom Turkey around Thanksgiving.

Although the friendship between a white child and an older black couple was an unlikely combination, it became a bridge that closed the gap in an all too prejudiced society. With wisdom, humility, and a servant's heart, Pickitt was able to give gifts through me to my family without it resembling charity. The treats he brought me from town provided moments of anticipation and joy. Knowing a turkey was being raised just for me told me I was loved and valued; it gave me a feeling of self-worth. It also gave me something to look forward to. I could not have known at the time all I was being taught. But somehow, I think Betty and Pickitt did. I also believe they were wise enough to learn simple lessons from a child too.

Tucked away inside this now grown-up heart is a childhood memory that causes a smile to escape every time I remember my special friends. Strange as it may seem, one of the first things I want to do when I get to heaven is look up Betty and Pickitt. I have a feeling their mansion will be easy to find. I'll just look for the smoke curling from their chimney and follow my nose to their door where I know, inside, sweet potatoes will be cooking in an old wood stove. I expect a kind and gentle face will greet me and say, "Why Miss Suzie, we've been waiting for you, Sugar. Come on in and let me fix you a plate."

But the wisdom that is from above is first pure,
then peaceable, gentle, and easy to be entreated,
full of mercy and good fruits,
without partiality, and without hypocrisy.
James 3:17 KJV

Chicken Nugget

Southern Fried Sweet Potatoes

Bake sweet potatoes in regular or microwave oven until done. Cool and put in refrigerator for several hours or overnight. Peel cold sweet potatoes and slice with knife. Pour cooking oil in skillet and heat. Place sweet potato slices in hot oil, and turn once, cooking until slightly brown. Drain on paper towel and serve warm with a sprinkle of salt and brown sugar.

CHAPTER 24

A Light in the Incubator

by Fran Caffey Sandin

Growing up on an East Texas farm, I remembered how new or sick baby chicks were often placed in an incubator. The light provided warmth, protection, and healing for the vulnerable little creatures. Now I felt like the wounded chick, the one who needed encouragement and protection. While life had held some happy and funny times for me, this was not one of them. I wished I could crawl into the incubator, but it seemed the light had been turned off. What could I do?

Recovering from a back injury, I lay prone on the family room floor. But the physical pain paled in comparison to the emotional devastation I felt following my father's recent death. *God, where are You?* I felt abandoned—as though He had pulled a black shade. I could not see His face, feel His presence, or even imagine His goodness. Warm, salty tears saturated tissue after tissue as I tried to comprehend the unbelievable events.

How could this be? Suicide happened in other families—not ours. Dad was our steady rock, our patriarch. We loved him so. The questions seemed unending and the answers elusive. After being depressed for several months, Dad had taken a gun he had purchased for protection—and shot himself at home. Mother was the one who found him. How would she ever begin to deal with the shock, let alone the gut-wrenching disappointment of losing a lifelong mate? Suddenly, everything in my world seemed very dark. I had walked down a similar shadowy path years earlier while recovering from the death of our 17-month-old son Jeffrey. But now, it seemed I was tiptoeing over the grim and gloomy stones as if it were the very first time.

As I lay alone, facedown on a quiet Sunday morning, my husband and college-bound son and daughter were at church. Ordinarily I would have been playing the organ for the worship service, but this time I was in no physical, mental, or spiritual condition to lead others in worship.

Between sobs, I thought about Dad. I could almost smell the gasoline fumes emanating from his sturdy, twill work clothes. Coming home every day from his auto mechanic shop, he reeked of exhaust fumes and petroleum. I recalled how Dad had prayed fervently before every meal. His authoritative voice gave me security. At the dinner table, I always noticed his rough hands and oil-stained nails. Yet the softness, the gentleness of his hazel eyes, seemed more indicative of his heart. He was an honest, hard-working man, a veteran of World War II, a man who always placed the needs of others above his own. Many times he stayed late and labored long into the night helping a stranded motorist get on his way.

None of us realized how much Dad depended upon his career for his mental and emotional well-being. After his retirement, he became clinically depressed. He seemed even more downhearted while watching the live television coverage of the 1990-91 Persian Gulf War. What had he been thinking about or, posssibly, remembering?

Although Dad was under medical supervision, neither Mother, my brother, sister, nor I detected the depth of his illness. I longed to tell Dad how much I loved him, thank him for all his hard work, and shower him with words of appreciation and praise. Now I couldn't do that. Would the pain ever subside? I felt guilty for not understanding Dad's distress, anger toward God for letting him die, and a senselessness about all of it. *What happened, Lord? What is life all about anyway? This was not supposed to be in my script!*

God must have translated my thoughts into prayers because an answer came. As I lay on the floor, my shaky faith matching my prone posture, I recalled a quote by the late Joseph Bayly: "Never forget in the darkness what you learned in the light." Having experienced the excruciating loss of several children, his words held sway.

In earlier times, when my outlook was brighter, I remembered reading that God's Word is a lamp for my feet and a light to my path (Psalm 119:105). So I started reading a few passages each day from the Psalms—those familiar "songs in the night" that have comforted countless others. Gradually, I began to feel that God understood my questions and my pain; and that He truly cared for me. Over a period of time, I felt God's love covering me like a warm bandage, and His Word became the light in my darkened incubator.

Adjusting to my dad's death was not easy. But through a process of time, with many ups and downs, I gradually regained my equilibrium and zest for life. This wounded chick began to heal and actually became stronger as a result of the ordeal. God's words seemed to leave the pages of the Bible and bury themselves deep within my soul. Like a balm, they comforted me and gave me the hope and encouragement I needed day by day.

Because of God's Word, now I know—not just in my head, but deep down in my heart—that God's there in the sunshine, but He draws especially near to His hurting chicks as they stumble in the dark.

For I am convinced that neither death, nor life, nor angels,
nor principalities, nor things present, nor things to come,
nor powers, nor height, nor depth, nor any other created
thing, shall be able to separate us from the love of God,
which is in Christ Jesus our Lord.
Romans 8:38-39 NASB

Chicken Nugget

Ten Ways You Can Become a Channel of God's Love to a Grieving Friend

1. Take food to the home in disposable containers or send a gift certificate for a restaurant meal or takeouts.
2. Take a sack of paper goods and plastic ware. Include a can of coffee or some tea bags.
3. If children are involved, take a plate of cookies or a small gift just for them. Offer to keep children for an evening if that would be helpful.
4. Pay for a hotel room for out-of-town relatives.
5. Go to the home and offer to answer the door and the telephone. Help with household chores.
6. Let her know that you are praying for her. Send a card or small gift.
7. Give your time. Sit with her, listen to her, cry with her.
8. Mark the date of her loss on your calendar. Several months later, take her to lunch.
9. Remember special days during the first year— especially the anniversary of the death of a loved one, and holidays; call or write a note.
10. Give her lots of hugs.

CHAPTER 25

Fried, Tried, and Chickened Out

by Susan Duke

I watched the sun as it slowly drifted down behind the masses of oak and cedar trees. My old rocking chair creaked to the rhythmic chirps of a nearby cricket companion as I gently rocked on my back porch. The sunshine warmed my spirit as well as my face and bare feet on that crisp autumn afternoon. I smiled, silently thanking the sun for letting me view its spectacular display of beauty. Suddenly awed by the moment, I asked myself, *How long has it been since I allowed myself the treat of such a simple indulgence?* My heart whispered the answer: *Too long.*

Had it not been for the serenity that enveloped me at that moment, I might have felt guilty, guilty for the declaration I had made just the day before. I even wondered if God might be mad at me for saying, "Lord, I quit! Where do I go to resign?" I could only hope He understood my heart. I was "chickening out" of all the things that kept me so busy for God and resigning from all religious facades—but not from my love for Him.

Somehow, this did not feel like the other times in the past when I had experienced the repercussions of "burnout" from going too much and keeping an overfilled calendar. I'd been fried and tried before—exhausted both physically and mentally. A brief getaway would usually recharge my batteries and get me back in routine. But this was different—something inside seemed to be calling me into unknown territory, to a journey deeper than any I'd traveled before, beginning on the day I was drawn to the sunshine and sanctuary of my porch.

I felt emptied that afternoon, yet so settled and still, and I sensed I would be occupying this "waiting place" for some time. Something was changing inside my soul, and it felt more right than anything had felt in a very long time. For now, I had only one goal in mind: solitude.

Evidently, God took me at my word about resigning. After months of frenzied activity, my phone abruptly stopped ringing. For three months I didn't pencil in a single speaking or singing engagement. I felt distanced from friends and relatives. Good sermons and even music, which I always loved, did not move me. Though everything had quieted in my world, I wasn't depressed. As a matter of fact, I felt an uncanny resolve to embrace this time which, for whatever reason, had come to my soul. I instinctively knew I needed this season of silence.

I had been far too busy for the past few years; at the same time I'd been recovering from a traumatic season of grief. But this was not the only reason I'd told the Lord, "I quit." To be honest, I simply had become disillusioned with much of what I had come to know as "ministry." It seemed that every church I knew anything about was in trouble—discord among the members, financial woes and worries, misplaced priorities over building projects, names on pews, and on and on. It seemed as though the ladders being climbed by the church world were hardly different from the ones being scaled in the corporate world. I remember contemplating about this one day as I cried out, "Lord, do You even see what is being done in Your name?"

Author and teacher, Malcolm Smith, once told a story about an encounter he had with a pastor friend. He was surprised, after not seeing him for a few years, to find that the man was no longer a minister. His friend simply stated that he had found more love in the local bar than he had ever found in church. *How sad*, I thought. *But how often, so true.*

One day, while meeting with a woman who had a speaking ministry, I asked, "How are things going?" Expecting to hear about the blessing of sharing and lives being changed, I felt my heart sink when, instead, she described her ministry in terms of how it was doing financially and the latest strategy for securing bookings. I couldn't help but think of a simple children's story I'd once read.

Hope for the Flowers, by Tina Paulus, is about two caterpillars named Stripe and Yellow. Before spinning their own cocoons, the two spent all their time climbing up a great column with other squirming and pushing caterpillars. In their frantic rush, they were finally faced with two options: climb up or be climbed upon. No one knew what was at the top of the column, but "getting there" seemed to be the big goal of caterpillar life.

Growing disenchanted with crawling up, Stripe and Yellow became still. Soon they found themselves at the bottom of the pile where they were free to spin cocoons—cocoons that would eventually give them wings. They discovered that having wings was really the only way to get to the top. Stripe and Yellow actually made their greatest progress while they were being still.

We can learn a lot from Stripe and Yellow. We humans get so easily caught up in programming and formulating our lives that, sometimes, we miss our real purpose. Perhaps we need to make inward journeys rather than outward, visible climbs. One of the most powerful, but least observed, verses in the Bible is found in Psalm 46:10: "Be still and know that I am God."

I learned more in those three months of waiting and resting than I'd learned at any other time in my life. I discovered the simplicity of God's love and the gift of delight He gives us in small moments—working in my garden, sitting on my porch, or walking through the woods. Simple prayers of thanksgiving rose in my heart every time I saw a butterfly or a leaf dancing in the wind. My soul was at play with all of God's creation, and in the hush of morning, I could almost hear His heartbeat.

William Blake penned these words: "To see the world in a grain of sand, and heaven in a wild flower, hold infinity in the palm of your hand—and eternity in an hour." Even the words to a cherished Christmas carol took on new meaning to me. "Joy to the world . . . let heaven and nature sing." Perhaps for a time, my soul needed to be still enough to hear only the songs that heaven and nature sing. In that stillness, I began to truly understand the wonders of His love. In resting, my soul was growing up.

Toward the end of the three months of quiet, I began to approach God like a little girl saying, "I don't know much, Lord. But I know I love You." Suddenly knowing less, seemed more. In the movie, *Forrest Gump*, Forrest was always successful in reaching his goal because he stayed focused and kept his goals simple. I was learning to embrace a Gump-like outlook on life.

Turning on the radio in my car one day, I caught only the last few words of a sermon. Words, I know I was supposed to hear.

"Would you like to know what this unusual period of time you've been experiencing has been about?" the preacher asked. "It's called *Selah,* which means to stop. It doesn't mean to stop and do something else; it just simply means stop. One day you will find out what this stopping place has been about and realize that God has a plan. It may seem irrelevant right now, but God is changing you and preparing you for a new phase of growth and service."

Four years have passed since my *Selah* and Stripe-and-Yellow time, and if I knew who the preacher was who voiced those words of wisdom that day, I'd tell him he hit this chick's nail on the head. God did have a plan. After the period of resting, my calendar grew full again, but not so full I couldn't enjoy a crimson sunset from my back porch, and not so full that I couldn't occasionally stop and pick some wildflowers along a country road.

I came to understand what T. S. Elliot meant when he wrote the phrase, "A lifetime burning in every moment." I learned to actually lie down in green pastures, and I let God lead me beside the still waters where I could see a reflection of His love in simple things I had once taken for granted. I learned that all of our doing will serve Him and others better when we first learn the art of being.

I emerged from my chrysalis feeling as if I'd had a long, soaking bath in a tub full of God's love. Resting and letting the Lord rejuvenate my spirit was vital in this transition period.

Now, I could hardly wait to get back to work and share with others what I'd learned. My metamorphosis was amazing. Even my shoulders felt different.

Could it be . . . that this chicken was sprouting a pair of butterfly wings?

The heavens declare the glory of God; the skies proclaim the
work of his hands. Day after day they pour forth speech;
night after night they display knowledge. There is no speech
or language where their voice is not heard. Their voice goes
out into all the earth, their words to the ends of the world.
Psalm 19:1-4

Chicken Nugget

Simple Things

Teddy bears and rocking chairs
are some of my favorite things.
Cookie jars and shooting stars,
and robins in the spring.
Fields of flowers and April showers;
velvet grass beneath bare feet;
Gentle rain on windowpanes,
and ice cream sundae treats.
Country folks and silly jokes,
lazy summer afternoons,
Porch swings and songs to sing
and roses in full bloom.
Autumn leaves, a crisp cool breeze,
a golden harvest moon;
A fireplace, a cozy fire,
a guitar with a simple tune,
Candlelight and winter nights,
long letters from a friend.
Cinnamon smells and fairy tales,
old quilts to snuggle in.
Fireflies and apple pies,
the laughter of a child.
Believing all things are possible,
and that even angels smile.
Simple things are favorite things—
gifts from God above—
Priceless treasures money can't buy—
acquired through hearts of love.

SECTION IV

Perched in High Places
Confidence in Overcoming Obstacles

CHAPTER 26

Little Red-Faced Hen

by Becky Freeman

I thought all family reunions proceeded like ours. First comes the food. In the Jones' family, sugar was always our main course. Oh, someone may have baked some little pitiful looking bird or square of canned ham, but none of us really considered that the main course. (I'll never forget five-year-old cousin Kenny asking my mother, "What kind of chicken is this, Aunt Ruthie? Turkey?") But the dessert table was always where the spectacular food was. To a child's hungry eyes, it seemed at least a mile long.

Once we had our fill of sugar and caffeine, aunts, uncles, cousins, grandmas, and grandpas would stumble into the living room for the third course: storytelling. More specifically, we gathered together to tell the most embarrassing thing that had happened to us in the previous year. One year my cousin Jamie brought the house down describing her experience going to the funeral of someone she had loved and admired. She discovered, once she was seated on the front row and the eulogy was in progress, that she was at the funeral of the wrong person. She had to feign being overcome with grief in order to escape.

My mother always came to these family sessions fully loaded (with stories, that is). One of my all-time favorite true tales occurred one morning as my mother sat on the porch drinking her coffee. Suddenly a middle-aged woman walked into view. The strange woman, as mother tells it, was wearing a lime-green bikini—sporting fur-lined boots on her feet. She stopped to chat with mother and in the course of the rather awkward conversation, the woman let my mom know that she owned her own business.

"Now, I've learned one thing," the woman told mother proudly, "I don't hire pretty women. Men can't keep their minds on their work with pretty young things around the office. No, sir. I like to hire ugly, old women." Now my mother is a beautiful woman—inside and out—but she had been caught on this particular morning without benefit of makeup to face or brush to hair. At this point, the bikini-clad woman stopped mid-sentence, took a long look at Mother, sized her up carefully, then paid my mom the supreme compliment. "I'd hire you," she said.

I've lost count of how many times I've heard that story as I was growing up, and I'm still chuckling about it thirty years later. Actually, I was a mother with children of my own before it occurred to me that telling embarrassing stories isn't a part of every family's legacy and tradition.

Pity.

For if you grow up knowing that an embarrassing moment can be redeemed into a hilarious story by the year's end, the pain of being mortified gives way to the joy of being a ham. If I have been gifted in this life, I believe it is to have survived more red-faced moments than anyone else on the planet—and still live to tell the tale. Over and over and over again. As a matter of fact, I got so proficient at stumbling into embarrassing situations and telling about them later that eventually I had no choice but to turn it into an income-producing venture.

Nearing midlife, I've survived nearly every conceivable form of embarrassment. I've fallen from platforms—face up and face down.

I've unknowingly carried a bag of trash, dangling it daintily from my arm, up and down a crowded mall—believing all the while I was carrying my purse.

I've been shopping for clothes and noticed a sudden chill beneath my waist, then realized—with a start—that my wraparound skirt had come unwrapped.

I've called my husband home to help me retrieve my keys from a locked car—only to discover that the driver's side window had been rolled completely down the entire time.

I've put eye shadow on my lips and lipstick on my eyelids. Spray starched my hair, and hair sprayed my blouses.

On the day of my teacher evaluation (during my short stint as a first grade teacher), I showed up for work—much to my own shock—wearing one red shoe and one black one. (I think I got extra marks for "creativity" on my evaluation form!)

At one embarrassing—but very memorable—athletic event, I volunteered to carry a five-gallon container of orange Kool-Aid to the concession stand. Only problem was, with every step across the length of the field, I unwittingly pressed the spigot against my abdomen. I started out the morning dressed mostly in white; I ended up the day wearing mostly orange drink.

You may ask, "Is there no end to these stories?"

No, there is no end.

Then there was the day the elementary principal asked me to come in to discuss my son's problems with his organizational skills and how I might help him "just generally get his act together." After the conference with the principal, I assured her I'd help "get my son together." I walked out of the office and caught a glimpse of my reflection in the office window. My embarrassment blossomed into full red-faced bloom when I realized I'd been reassuring the principal—with a forgotten curler bobbing atop the center of my head.

Need I go on?

I need.

Cars have turned out to be quite the popular vehicle for supplying me with embarrassing material. I've driven off with gasoline pump handles. Absconded with those little bank tubes more times than I can count. I've plowed into so many of our neighbor's mailboxes that my husband keeps several spares on hand. Once a band of teenagers went on one of those reckless sprees, plowing down every mailbox in the neighborhood. The next morning as I drove my children to school they observed with mouths agape, all the mailboxes lying on the ground or bent awkwardly at the middle. In unison, my own children accusingly chided, "Mother! How could you!"

I once drove backwards for five miles—in full view of my bewildered neighbors—because I couldn't get my car to go forward. (This threw several dogs into a state of confusion. They so wanted to chase my car—but which way to run?)

It's not like I only have old stories to tell either. God graciously keeps me with a fresh supply of public humiliation to choose from. Last week, for example, I was on a television show. Felt pretty good about myself, I did. I was poised, relaxed, and my hair and makeup looked extra nice. As I was relating this very thing to my husband after the show he kept looking at me intently as if trying to swallow a smile. Finally I blurted, "What? What is it?"

"Becky," Scott said, as kindly as possible, "it's just that there's a—" Before he finished his sentence he reached over and plucked a two-inch long black hair from my chin. I'd gone on national TV dangling a two-inch long hair from the tip of my chin. (Where is Gracie's tweezer-toting mother when you need her?)

But the worst, the absolute worst and most embarrassing moment I've ever survived is now known far and wide as The Window Story. I share it again here for those of you who may not have yet read it over the Internet or heard it whispered across the neighbor's fences.

I had been reading books about spicing up a midlife marriage and was anxious to try out some of the ideas. One night as I was exiting from the shower wrapped in a towel, I saw the lights of my husband's pickup pull up in the driveway. It was the perfect opportunity. Since we lived in a remote area, I felt quite safe in trying out my idea—guaranteed to spice up a sagging love life.

I struck a pose at our bedroom window, dropped my towel, and gave my husband the best come hither look I could come up with. I heard lots of excited noises outside the window, and assuming I had hit on something Scott really appreciated, I responded in kind. A few seconds later there was a knock at the bedroom door. It was Scott. He peeked in the room and announced, "Hi, Hon, I'm home! And guess what? Gary is with me." Gary was my best friend's husband.

I was in embarrassment recovery for the better part of that month.

Yes, I am an "embarrassment survivor"—of the highest order. When people compare the things they've done with my list of embarrassing scenes, they inevitably back down and admit, "Yes, Becky, you are the Queen of the Red-Faced Moment."

To which I humbly respond, "Well, it's a living."

She can laugh at the days to come.
Proverbs 31:25

Chicken Nugget

"Oooops, I Made a Boo-Boo"
Real-life Classified Ads
(Author Unknown)

Lost: small apricot poodle. Reward.
Neutered. Like one of the family.

Four-poster bed, 101 years old.
Perfect for antique lover.

We do not tear your clothing with machinery.
We do it carefully by hand.

Great Dames for sale.

Stock up and save! Limit: one.

Tired of cleaning yourself? Let me do it.

Dog for sale: eats anything and is fond of children.

CHAPTER 27

Flying the Coop and Sailing Away

by Fran Caffey Sandin

"Me? Sailing? You're kidding!" That was my first response when Jim told me he wanted to learn sailing. He's a naval history buff, and I thought he'd just been reading too many books about the ocean. But when his desire did not fade, reality hit. My husband would soon be a captain, and I would be his first mate.

Frankly, I was chicken. The wildest water adventure this hen ever had was riding the log ride at Six Flags. And to be quite honest, I've never liked getting my feathers wet. I could swim a little, but not well enough to stay afloat in a sea of waves. A sinking feeling in the pit of my gizzard emerged as I envisioned myself marching across the gangplank to the ominous ship. I'd be wearing a giant life preserver, clutching a seasickness pill in one hand and a bucket in the other.

During our 12 years of marriage, we'd always enjoyed tackling new projects together. Why make this an exception? As I watched Jim pouring over all the sailing brochures, I thought, *He is like a boy with a new toy. I can't be a wet hen and dampen his enthusiasm now.* So I smiled bravely as we packed our bags for the week-long sailing school in Hilton Head, South Carolina.

The morning of our first lesson I felt nervous but wanted to look like a professional "sailswoman." After greeting Jim with a good morning kiss, I dressed for the day—immaculate white slacks with a new blue and white polo shirt—gave myself an approving glance in the mirror, and set out for school. As we headed down the path toward the pier, I jauntily skipped along on Jim's port side. The fresh ocean breeze against my cheeks temporarily calmed my quaking gullet.

An older seafaring couple was sitting on a park bench along the sidewalk, and I couldn't help noticing how the woman scrutinized me as we passed. With leathery skin and hair like a broom, she puffed on a cigarette. Her wry smile and the twinkle in her eye should have clued me in.

Later that morning, we recognized her bearded and tattooed husband as Buster, the authentic old salt who was to be our instructor on the 28-foot racing boat, the *Soling*. Buster explained that our vessel was guaranteed not to turn over. With a sigh of relief, I was ready to raise the sails, lay back, and enjoy the ride. Buster had other plans. He assigned each one of us a task, and I quickly learned to "crew."

Soon my head was spinning from all the nautical terms: Ready about? Hard-a-lee! Jibe-Ho! Watch out for the Boom! Each time the *Soling* rolled from side to side, I lost my footing. Even though I tried to stay balanced, I slipped around the cockpit off and on all day. Forget "crewing," I felt like crowing instead—for my old comforting land-bound coop.

By the time we sailed back to port, my hair looked like a mop (to match Mrs. Buster's broom); my smudged-with-mud polo shirt and spiffy white pants resembled a zebra's coat.

Buster beamed as he assisted me from the boat, "See ya in the mornin'."

"Sure," I groaned, choking back tears.

As Jim and I trudged toward the condo, Buster's wife watched intently, enjoying every minute. Between laughs, she squawked with a coarse voice, "Hey, try a little Clorox, Honey!" *How embarrassing.* I'd certainly confirmed my inexperience to Mrs. Buster that morning. She must have pegged me as an amateur on my crisp, white, jaunty way out to sea. My disheveled appearance confirmed it on the way back to land.

I attempted a sheepish grin in her direction, but didn't feel at all like smiling. The first day of sailing was not glamorous, not at all like the gorgeous magazine pictures I'd seen. It was *work.* Dirty, tired, and nauseated, I sported rope burns on both hands, two broken fingernails, and was sore and wobbly as well.

When we reached the condo, I made a valiant effort to walk up the stairs, but when my legs gave out about halfway up, I began pulling myself along the banister with the waning strength in my arms. Stumbling into the bedroom, I flopped across the bed and wondered, *Will this hen* ever *sail again?*

Early the next morning Jim bounced out of bed eager for Lesson Two. Determined to be a good sport, I pulled on a pair of old jeans, forced a smile, stretched my aching muscles, and prayed for a better day.

The remainder of the week held both rewarding and scary experiences, but when Buster handed me my graduation certificate, I felt like a heroine in one of those seagoing adventure novels. As I continued to embrace my husband's dream, it eventually became mine too. Now we've become quite the team. Jim is the brave Cap'n of our vessel—and me?

I'm the romantic first mate with a carefree hairdo, hands leisurely tucked into pockets (now stuffed with chewing gum instead of seasickness pills), and an ear tuned to the Captain's voice—ready to "crew" upon command.

I've discovered that the quiet swish of the boat cutting through the water soothes my soul. Being out on the blue water under a sky full of fluffy clouds refreshes my spirit and renews my energy. Away from the hassles of life, Jim and I enjoy lazy discussions about life and our future goals. We've found that spending time with each other requires planning and determination on both our parts. Otherwise, it's the first item left out in our busy schedules.

Even though the initial idea of sailing was terrifying and the lessons hard, I'm so glad I found the courage to learn something new. Now when my rooster wants to sail away, this former chicken says, "Aye, Aye, Cap'n—let's fly this coop, hit the water, and go have some fun!"

I can do all things through Him who strengthens me.
Philippians 4:13 NASB

Confidence for Chickens with Wobbly Sea Legs

Chicken Nugget

Psalm 107:23,25-31:
Others went out on the sea in ships. . . .
A tempest . . . lifted high the waves. . . .
In their peril their courage melted away.
They reeled and staggered like drunken men;
they were at their wits' end.
Then they cried out to the LORD in their troubles,
and he brought them out of their distress.
He stilled the storm to a whisper;
the waves of the sea were hushed.
They were glad when it grew calm,
and he guided them to their desired haven.
Let them give thanks to the LORD
for his unfailing love.

Psalm 27:1,3:
The LORD is my light and my salvation—
whom shall I fear?
The LORD is the stronghold of my life—
of whom shall I be afraid?
Though an army besiege me, my heart will not
fear; though war break out against me,
even then will I be confident.

CHAPTER 28

Something Stuck in My Craw

by Gracie Malone

In concert with the rising sun, our red bantam rooster fluttered from his perch in a nearby tree and strutted about the yard loudly proclaiming the morning. Joe and I hopped out of bed, stripped the sheets, stuffed them in the washing machine, whirled it in gear, and headed for the kitchen. As Joe poured coffee, our son, Jason, stumbled toward the refrigerator.

It was a typical Monday, until I heard water gurgling in the downstairs bathroom. Bounding the stairs to turn off the washer, I shouted, "Septic tank's stopped up again! Call Roto-Rooter!"

"Oh, no," Joe countered, "that costs too much! I'll rent a rooter."

I groaned as Joe hopped in his car and headed to town. Driving back home after dropping Jason off at school I thought, *Why did I wait until today to prepare tomorrow's Bible study lesson?*

Gravel popped beneath my wheels as I pulled in the driveway and stepped on the brakes. Joe was dressed in a business suit, white shirt, and tie. Beside him a robotic sewer machine stood at attention like a soldier reporting for duty. It had a round belly of coiled cable, an arm-like appendage jutting out on one side, and a fearsome hand-shaped claw. My chicken-heart fluttered nervously.

"Will you help me?" Joe asked as I stepped from my car. "It'll only take a minute." He smiled optimistically as he stooped to examine the black hole he'd made in the septic line. As he proceeded to stuff the robot's arm into its dark recesses, I, being a good wife, answered, "Sure."

Joe showed me a big red metal button connected to an electrical line that powered the robot. My simple task, explained Joe, was to step on the button when he said "Go" and step off when he said "Stop."

"No problem," I nodded in the affirmative and stepped up to do my duty.

"Go," Joe said. I stomped on the switch. Joe patiently guided the robot's arm as it inched its way into the clogged line. As the motor droned rhythmically, my mind shifted gears, thinking of the loftier pursuits waiting in my cozy study.

"Stop!" Joe shouted.

I did stop, but apparently not soon enough. In horror, I watched the cable backlash around Joe's leg, leaving traces of black muck on his trousers.

"Pay attention!" Joe yelled. Then with a pained look in his eyes, he added, "Gracie, you're not interested in our septic system, are you?"

"I love our septic tank!" I responded in quick defense.

While Joe untangled the cable, I noticed a chill in the air and rubbed at the goose bumps popping up on my arms.

"Hon," I said, "I'm going to leave my post—for just a minute—and run get a coat." I dashed inside, flung open the folding closet doors, grabbed a jacket, gave the doors a shove, and whirled around. Before I could slip my arm in the sleeve, one door pivoted and fell, whacked my head, then bounced and landed in a crippled heap on the floor. As I walked back outside, warm tears made trails down my dust-covered cheeks. A small goose egg throbbed on my crown. "The sky is falling!" I wailed as I walked toward Joe with open arms. "The closet door just fell on my head!"

Joe held and comforted me, wiping my tears with the back of his cleanest hand. He stifled a laugh, and when I realized it really was pretty funny, we both gave in to a chuckle. Assured that I was consoled and in control of my emotions, Joe turned back to the business at hand. He reinserted the robot's arm into the gaping hole while mumbling, "The joys of country livin'!"

After working one full hour, the claw reached the blockage and gouged its way through unseen mire. I went inside to clean the bathroom only to hear Joe call out, "Gracie, would you help me re-hang the closet door?"

I met him at the entry hall, and we began our struggle with the complicated door. I stooped to work on the bottom part while Joe attempted to place the top roller back in its track—a difficult task, even on a good day. Joe would get his roller in track and the bottom pin would bounce out. I'd get the pin at the bottom snug, and Joe's roller would jump the track. Before long, Joe bellowed in exasperation, "Bend closer to the floor so you can see!"

Obediently, I got down on all fours. My position was a bit "squawkward," but I had to admit, I had a better view of what needed to be done.

"Push to the right," I said. Joe obediently complied. Unfortunately, what I really meant to say was "Push to the left!" When Joe looked down, all he could see was my startled face— pinched between the wooden facing and the dangling door.

"You don't love me!" I wailed.

"Yes I do!" he responded, then with a wink he added, "Even more than I love our septic system."

Eventually we managed to get the door on track—and my face dislodged and patted to its original shape. Joe changed clothes, then sheepishly grinned as he asked, "How 'bout giving me a hand one more time? Just for fun."

Hand in hand, we bravely marched outside to face "Rooter-D-2." Joe placed the robot behind the car's bumper and gave me instructions on how to lift it. Then, with deep feeling in his voice, he put his arms around my shoulders and said, "No matter what happens when we pick this thing up, I do love you."

We put the machine into the trunk without doing bodily injury or emotional harm, and I headed inside to clean up the mess. It looked like a mother hen with her brood of chicks had been scratching for worms in the mud on the floor.

The time I'd planned for doing Bible study was more than half gone. *If I can just collect my emotions before another disaster strikes,* I thought, *I'll be a happy woman.* But lo, it was not to be.

Before I could find the mop, Joe called from the back door, "Gracie, I need you to take me to work. My car won't start!"

Do not boast about tomorrow, for you do not know
what a day may bring forth.
Proverbs 27:1

Chicken Nugget

Stress-busters

1. Spend a few quiet moments alone with God.
2. Take a stroll around the barnyard (or the block).
3. Tuck your head under your wing for a nap.
4. Roost in a porch swing with a book of poems.
5. Praise the Lord often for all His blessings.
6. Get together with a few good hens.
7. Have a cup of "eggs-presso" or vanilla hazelnut coffee.
8. Drive the country backroads enjoying pastoral scenes.
9. Be early to roost in the evening.
10. See a "chick flick."

CHAPTER 29

I'll Fly Away

by Rebecca Barlow Jordan

If only the other wives could see me now, I thought, as I entered the discount department store. My faded shorts, stained blouse, and lopsided thongs hardly resembled my "image" of an ideal pastor's wife. But this was urgent—no time to worry about fashion or peers. *God will have to pull a miracle out of His hat for me this evening!* I was to attend our first deacon/wife leadership meeting, one I had helped plan. My job was to teach the women. *What can I possibly tell them?* I thought. *I'm the one who needs help!*

An unruly curl flopped over my warped sunglasses. I raised one side of my specs and peeked out, quickly scanning the store for familiar faces. Safe. I brushed away a conspicuous tear, sighed, and marched over to the sales counter.

"Can you tell me where there's a park with a lake around it? I . . . I know I've seen one around here somewhere," I stammered to the store clerk.

She repeated the directions three or four times at my request. "You're not far from the lake."

"Thank you," I whispered, turning away before the clerk could see my next wave of fresh tears.

I was used to crying. A 42-hour labor, and several weeks of only three hour-a-night sleeps after the birth of my first baby, had left me anything but laughing. I was exhausted and my doctor said all I needed was rest. "Don't answer the phone," he advised. So I tried that. But one night I forgot his order and absently picked up the receiver.

"Hello, Rebecca?" It was my brother's voice.

My words popped out like marbles in a pinball machine: "Can't talk now! I think this egghead is cracking up." I'm sure after my phone greeting, my brother probably thought I might be losing a few marbles.

During those two months of what I began to understand was postpartum depression, it seemed as if I would shatter into a hundred pieces, like a fragile eggshell. And like Humpty Dumpty, I was afraid no one could put me back together again. However, in the weeks that followed as my baby began to sleep through the night and I got more sleep, sanity and normalcy began to return to my life.

Then a decade later, my emotional roller coaster began again. Intermittent bouts with severe PMS (I often called it "premonster syndrome") often plunged me to the depths of depression. Sometimes in crowds, panic took over. I felt like a frozen chicken placed into a 400 degree oven—without the chance to first thaw. The shock of the heat wave sent my wilted wings scrambling for cover. However, I stubbornly refused to let down my feathers to anyone—except my Heavenly Father. I thought no one else would understand, so I nestled under His wings, poured out my chicken heart, and waited out the storms by myself.

In addition, overcommitments, "SuperMom" delusions, and self-imposed expectations about being in the ministry had plucked my physical energy and left me emotionally disabled—

(All right, *more* emotionally disabled.) For several years, spiritual strength oozed out unintentionally, creating a vacuum for resentment and unforgiveness to creep in. Living in a glass henhouse had finally taken its toll.

As I drove down the road, my thoughts returned to the present, and I realized I had missed the turn leading to the park. For over half an hour, I wandered around like a chicken with its head cut off. Finally, I squawked in exasperation, "Lord, this is not funny. I can't even find the place I want to run away to!"

A flash of white feathers darted into view. "The ducks! The ducks! There it is!" As I pulled into the parking lot, I must have sounded like a child on her first visit to the zoo. A family of quacking fowl waddled in front of me, lined up for a hot summer's splash. I found a quiet, shady spot beside the man-made lake and plopped my Bible and notebook down on the faded, rickety picnic table. I took a deep breath, preparing for my own pity party—and hopefully for a bolt of truth from heaven. Only a few years before, I had nested here for a half-day, personal retreat—mapping out plans and dreams and swallowing whole nuggets of truth from God's Word. What a contrast to today's mission!

Glancing across the lake, I noticed its unusual muddy appearance. "That's what I feel like inside, God," I began to sob, "all clouded, confused, and muddy. I know You're here, but I don't hear You. I don't see You. I don't feel You! I really need some answers." I felt foolish crying out to God. Surely others needed Him more than I—yet I longed for healing and restoration.

I poured over the Psalms, my familiar retreat. David's songs had soothed my silent wails and wistful yearnings on many occasions. Foolish, unrestrained worries and fears flew in and out, diverting my attention from His Word: *What will people think? What if I crack up with this depression? Won't squawking about my struggle hinder our ministry? I love my husband too much to disappoint him. After all a pastor's wife should stay on top of things.*

The noisy quacking of the ducks jolted me back to where I was. I noticed one particular duck trying to escape to the other side of the lake. Like the ugly duckling in the fairy tale I had read as a child, it was homely, a dull brown. The other white ducks taunted it, pecking away at its tail feathers. My body sagged, my emotions dragged, and I felt like that trapped duck—alone, bewildered, and eager to fly away. Unlike that bird, however, the flood of depression wouldn't roll off my "chicken" back. I was drowning, and I knew it.

The day passed quickly, and the Arizona sun warmed my body, but not my heart. God had given me no *rhema*, no personal words for me. In my heart, I knew God loved me. But in my spirit, I felt He had betrayed me. My family would soon return home from work and school, so I gathered my Bible and papers and trudged back to the car. "I cannot handle one more day, God," I cried. "Please help me."

I headed home in silence. *What are we going to tell them tonight, God?* About halfway home, I turned the radio on and heard a familiar tune. I listened with awed reverence, like a child drinking in the delights of Christmas. Heavenly strains of "My Father's Angels," one of Bill Gaither's older Gospel songs, poured into my spirit like a healing ointment. The message spoke of God's protective love through ministering angels, wherever we go.

Tears streamed unashamedly now—tears of joy—and I found myself genuinely smiling. The song had given me a revelation that His angels *were* around me—that they were behind me and before me—watching over me. I realized at that moment that God would never let me run too far away. He would heal my heart, restore my joy, and renew my energy. God was sufficient! It was *my* image that was distorted, not God's view of me. I felt a fresh wind of hope flutter over me, like the gentle brushing of heavenly wings.

That night, with a radiant glow, I shared my experience with the other ladies. "I ran away today," I said, unfolding the day's story. "But God's angels led me back home." That confession was a good beginning on the road to wholeness.

That was years ago. Gradually, I learned the healthy habit of squawking regularly to my husband and supportive friends. I no longer peck at myself or worry about others' *eggs-pectations* in the same destructive way. I am forever learning how to cope with life's imbalances. (But thankfully, PMS flew out when aging set in.)

I still run away occasionally—but now I've learned to run into the arms of my Heavenly Father who loves me and accepts me just as I am.

Oh, that I had wings.
I would fly away and be at rest.
Psalm 55:6

Chicken Nugget

His Nest Is Best

The Father has no favorites.
Each child is precious to Him.
His nest is never too full;
His table is never too small;
His arms are never too short
to embrace all—
who call Him "Daddy."

CHAPTER 30

A Travel Guide for Big Chickens

by Becky Freeman

A mere two or three years ago, I could have volunteered as a model for a picture of the "The Accident-Prone Tourist." I could have written a classic and titled it *Gullible's Travels*. I was not only terrified of flying in an airplane (often digging my fingernails into the arms of startled passengers sitting next to me), I was mortified by maps, intimidated by rental cars, and panicky at the thought of staying in a hotel all by myself. Having gone from depending on my parents, to depending on Scott when we married at seventeen, I had precious little experience in self-sufficiency. When my parents or my husband were not around, I, like Blanche from *A Streetcar Named Desire*, "depended on the kindness of strangers" to get me headed in the right direction.

I've certainly added up my share of travel bloopers. On a solo trip to Nashville, I parked my rental car in the gargantuan Opryland Hotel parking lot. The next morning when I strolled out to retrieve it, I could only remember one thing: my car was white. I had no idea where I had parked it the night before. I blinked as I surveyed the Opryland parking lot, generously dotted with hundreds of white vehicles.

With no other recourse, I walked up and down the endless aisles, testing my key in every white car door. After forty-five minutes of trying, I finally found "the winner." I half expected lights to flash, loud music to start up, and a game show host to come out and congratulate me.

On one of my maiden voyages alone, after alternately losing and finding my purse, my luggage, and my plane ticket, a stewardess kindly asked, "Is there anything I can do to help you?"

"Yes," I replied, feeling much like an overwhelmed child. "Could you hold my hand and go with me the rest of the way?"

Traveling with confidence has not come easy to this chicken flyer. But in time, as I put one shaky leg after another, my cup of courage began to fill. This old chick learned some new traveling tricks and today, I find it hard to believe I was ever frightened of traveling alone. It has turned out to be one of midlife's most surprising delights.

I recently returned from speaking in Indianapolis and marvel how my travel savvy has broadened. I packed my bags for the trip in less than an hour, drove over to Dallas/Fort Worth airport and parked my car—alone and with confidence. Wheeling my luggage with the air of a seasoned traveler, I boarded the plane and soared above clouds, thinking mostly about the beauty of the earth below (instead of which exit to use when the plane crashed). Like a teenager with newfound freedom, I could hardly wait to get behind the wheels of a freshly vacuumed vehicle at the rental car agency. I was ripe for adventure—couldn't wait to begin exploring downtown Indianapolis and the backroads (and outlet malls) of upper Indiana.

When I burst into my spacious hotel room at the downtown Embassy Suite, I let out a delighted squeal, fell down on the freshly made bed and exclaimed, "Maids! Hot baths! Room service! No phone, fax, or family! I'm alone—deliriously, happily, marvelously—*alone!*" When I discovered the hotel was connected to a mall that had three specialty coffee shops, a bookstore, and a Cinnabun bakery, I knew I was in hog heaven.

Literally.

For I had come to Indy to speak at a feed convention, coming face to face with eight people who held Ph.D.'s in Swine Nutrition. Until that moment, I didn't know there was a degree in pigs—a doctorate degree, no less. After a lovely time of sharing with my newfound chicken- and hog-feed friends, I took off to explore the cornfield-lined highways of Indiana. About 60 miles out of the city, I saw a sign on a barn offering "Farm Counseling." *So is this where chickens go for therapy,* I mused.

I grinned as I passed several small billboards advertising, "Sherrill's Eat Here and Get Gas Cafe." I couldn't believe all the fascinating sites I was free to see, the new places just waiting to be discovered: all because I've stopped chickening out and begun venturing out instead.

The best part of getting over my traveling fears is the blessing of meeting people from all over the country. On my last rainy Sunday in Indiana, I drove to see my brother in Elkhart, keeping my eyes peeled for a coffee shop where I could duck in for a roadway treat. I couldn't believe my good fortune when I spotted "My Favorite Muffin and Coffee Place." Then I saw that the shop closed at 4:00 and my watch read 4:10. Instinctively, I thrust my bottom lip out in a childlike pout.

At that point the store's owner opened the door and waved me in. As I fairly skipped to the door he said, "You looked so pitiful, and I always hate it when I get some place just as they're closing. Come on in and warm up." I made up my mind right then and there—Indianians are my kind of people.

Though I'm often on the receiving end of a blessing, there are also times when it feels almost like God is moving me around—like a strategic chess piece—and placing me in the path of others who need an encouraging word. My becoming more free and mobile has helped me learn to see myself as a traveling vessel of God's love. In a crowded eatery in Indianapolis, I experienced just such a moment.

I sat down in the only available seat next to a young woman who was staring rather blankly at her paper-wrapped burrito.

"How are you doing?" I asked, popping a crouton from my Caesar salad into my mouth. She was fine, she explained, but a little down about her job. "Oh," I began, the mother hen rousing in me, "what would you really like to do?"

"I don't want to tell you. It's silly. Nobody ever makes a living at it. I never met anyone, personally, who succeeded in the field."

"Come on, you can tell me," I persisted. "After all, I'm a stranger to you. You'll never see me again after we finish our lunch."

"OK. But don't laugh." Big pause. "I've always wanted to be a writer."

Boy, did this gal ever sit down at the right table! She couldn't believe it when I told her I was a published author who actually made a living with words (albeit it is often a meager living) and that I'd once been a young girl with nothing but a crazy, secret dream: to write. Her eyes grew moist with tears of joy. "I can't believe this," she said. "I've been having the worst day. God must have known how badly I needed this lift."

I smiled. "There's a phrase in an old '70s song by Chuck Girland called *Love Song* that says, 'We aren't quite a mountain, but He's moved us here to you.'" I drew in a breath and looked her full in the face. "Now, I'm not quite a mountain, but I really believe He moved me here to you—at this little table in this crowded mall. He must care about you an awful lot."

As we continued to chat, I discovered this young girl was new in her faith. Only a year before she'd been heading to her dorm room planning how she could commit suicide. Instead, she happened into a meeting of Christians. "They prayed for me, the 'confirmed campus skeptic,' and suddenly all my arguments against Christianity seemed like a handful of pebbles next to this mountain of God's love."

As I walked away from that lunchtime experience, all warm and glowing inside, I couldn't help praying, "Thank You, Father, for pushing me out of my homebody nest, and helping me to overcome my fears of traveling. Thanks for holding my hand every time I feel overwhelmed and afraid. Oh, what I would have missed if I stayed a scared chicken, instead of learning how to fly."

It's been two weeks now since my trip to Indy, and I'm feeling acclimated again to my everyday life back in Texas. At my son's football game last night, I was feeling around in a pocket of my jacket and pulled up something that felt oddly familiar. Turned out to be keys to that zippy little car I rented in Indy. I chuckled to think what the poor guy at Avis must have done when this ditsy Texan checked in her rental car, then absconded with the keys.

The truth is, I'm still having some problems remembering where I park my car—both at home and out of state. But I wonder if I could get extra Good Traveler points for doing better at keeping up with my keys?

> *Be strong and courageous. Do not be terrified;*
> *do not be discouraged, for the LORD your God*
> *will be with you wherever you go.*
> Joshua 1:9

Chicken Nugget

Becky's Tips for Chickens-to-go

1. Even if you don't get a rental car, ask for one of the agency's free maps; they are completely nonintimidating to map-impaired people.
2. Carry a small, portable compass to press on to the window of your car when driving around a new city.
3. Invest in lightweight luggage with lots of pockets and on wheels.
4. Save up for a couple of suits in a top quality, wrinkle-free material.
5. Stride Rite Shoe Store carries a phenomenal little all-purpose silicone shoe shiner. No mess, no fuss, just wipe the dry, silicone sponge over your shoes and, ta-dum, a perfect shine.

CHAPTER 31

Confessions of a Slow Roaster

by Fran Caffey Sandin

When I knocked on her door at 9:00 a.m., I found my friend Linda bustling around putting the finishing touches on her already perfect home. Everything was so orderly. No paper piles. No clutter. Her dinner was already simmering and, if that wasn't enough, she was as cute and perky as a chickadee too. As I observed her organizational skills, I couldn't help but wonder, *Was she born that way?*

As we shared a cup of tea, I felt jealous. At that time in the morning my eyes were barely open, and the kind of home improvement my coop really needed was a bulldozer. In contrast to Linda's lively flitting around, I didn't have a fast bone in my body. The closest I ever came to being associated with rapid movement was when they named a famous hurricane "Fran." Not only did I move slowly, I never seemed to reach the end of my "to-do" list. With the demands of small children, I always felt about five years behind schedule.

If my husband asked me, "When are you planning to clean the playroom?" I had a standard answer. I'd say, "I'm fixing to."

That was East Texas talk for "I'll get around to it one of these days."

Having a phlegmatic, laid-back temperament was not helpful at this point. As I recalled my family of origin, we never got in a hurry about anything. We didn't need to. Our town consisted of a grocery/gas station, a cattle auction barn, a beauty shop, a grade school and two churches. What more could we possibly want?

The slower pace of country living left our calendar's "urgent" column blank; and "the fast lane" was reserved for the tractor. As a girl, I much preferred playing the piano or reading a book than doing chores. Mother set a good example; she always kept our farmhouse neat and tidy. But to me, cleaning seemed intensely boring.

So when I married a man (from Chicago) whose Swedish grandmother had been a professional housekeeper (and whose mother had been as well-trained as his grandmother), I should have expected some feathers to fly. In fact, my husband is just as fastidious as his mother hen. A peek into his closet today would reveal his shirts lined up on one side in categories: short sleeves together, long sleeves together, all the slacks on one side, suits on the other side. His shoes are in a row so straight that the toes look as though they were lined up against a level.

On the other side of the room is another kind of closet. Mine. When I open my closet door, I generally stand two paces back and wait for the surprise. I never know what might fall out next! I have made some improvements, but in truth, having separate closets all these years has probably saved our marriage.

Not only do I move slowly, I think through everything I want to say before saying it. By the time I have rehearsed it and get the courage to speak, the conversation has moved on to a different topic and my contribution makes no sense. Even worse is when folks are telling jokes and, just when everyone else has finished laughing, I say, "Oh—I get it now!" slap my knee and start to chuckle. Alone. Only my dearest friends love me anyway.

One day while cleaning I discovered a little card with the Serenity Prayer written on it: "God, grant me the serenity to accept the things I cannot change, courage to change the things I can, and the wisdom to know the difference." And I began to wonder, *Is my slow pace something I have to accept or is it something I just need the courage to change?* Unsure, I prayed for wisdom.

My prayer went something like, "Dear Lord, I know most people pray for You to slow them down, but I am asking You to speed me up. If this is something I can change, give me the courage to do it. And if You want to give me an extra blessing— would You throw in some organizational skills, too?"

The next day I had an appointment in Dallas, and because of interstate highway construction, I chose to drive on the back roads. While listening to a cassette tape, my foot became lead on the gas pedal. Soon the reflection of flashing red lights in my rearview mirror caught my attention, and I pulled off to the right. The stone-faced officer approached my car as though I were some sort of fugitive. When he reached my window he said grimly, "May I see your license, Ma'am? You were speeding."

I smiled and said, "I sure was." For the first time in my life I got a speeding ticket! I wanted to jump out, hug the young man and say, "God answered my prayer!" Of course, I couldn't blame God for my offense, but I couldn't help but wonder if He was smiling, too. I paid the ticket and, for the first time, had to remind myself to be more watchful of the speed zones.

As I continued to pray for change, a few books and conferences helped me recognize some basic problems. One reason for my paper pileup was a paralyzing inability to make a decision about junk mail. With my merciful disposition, I wanted to help others. But when everyone from coast to coast wanted my help, all I could say was, "Help!" In one seminar I learned a neat trick: Handle today's mail today. It sounded so easy, but what a difference it made to decide right away to throw it away or place it in a designated basket.

I also discovered I'm a sentimental junkie. I save cards, letters, and even old candy wrappers and dying flowers— because it reminds me of someone's love. From the children's first artistic creations to greeting cards from occasions long gone, I had to force myself to throw a few things away.

Procrastination is another downfall. When I decided to "just do it"—get organized and become efficient—I had to concentrate on making a place for everything and when it was time to put it back, I had to make a conscious effort to put it back in its place—right then. That step alone has cut out a big amount of clutter in my life.

It has taken years, but as I stopped making excuses for my lack of organization, God has given me the wisdom to do things differently. I learned to grab the old hen by her beak, look in the mirror and say, "Look here, old chick, we're going to make a few changes"—to which I could almost hear the mirror say, "Well, it's about time."

For I am confident of this very thing,
that He who began a good work in you will perfect it
until the day of Christ Jesus.
Philippians 1:6 NASB

Hints from the (Almost) Hurricane Hen

Chicken Nugget

1. Keep a cleaning supply caddy in a convenient location for each bathroom.
2. Organize chores by clustering. Do repeat chores at the same time. For example, make multiple sandwiches and put some in the freezer. Cook two casseroles and put one in the freezer.
3. When doing laundry, fold clothes as you are pulling them out of the dryer; put them directly into the basket and take them to the designated place.
4. Buy a filing cabinet or even a milk crate—and set up files. "File, don't pile."
5. Organize errands and have one or two designated errand days.
6. Open the mail at the same place each day and have the trash can handy.
7. Pray for God's guidance early in the morning.

CHAPTER 32

When a Chicken Goes to Church

by Gracie Malone

Traditionally, the first day of the week is a day of rest. Not so for a chicken who wants to look her Sunday best when she goes to church; sometimes just "putting on my face" is too much for this old hen to handle.

On a recent Sunday morning I awoke with a headache and was barely into my second cup of coffee when the clock warned: Time to get dressed. I donned my best denim outfit, cleansed my face with cold cream, dabbed skin freshener into my pores, and began the painstaking process of applying makeup, all the while thinking, *My, what we hens won't do to make ourselves look presentable.*

I applied moisturizer, concealer, foundation, pink blush, two shades of taupe eye shadow, and a thin line of dark brown eyeliner. Then I loaded the mascara brush with dark brown mascara, applied one coat to the topside of my lashes, and started on the underside, when, for reasons unknown, I blinked. Poked that tiny brush-looking thing straight into my eye. In an effort to keep tears from spilling over onto my freshly made face I tried bugging my eyes and glaring at the ceiling—to no avail.

Salty tears ran down my cheeks, washing brown goop into all the wrinkles around my eyes, filling the bags underneath. When my vision cleared to the point where I could fully assess the damage, I saw I'd also managed to paint a large, brown "Z" on my eyelid.

Quickly, I dipped a Q-tip into eye-makeup remover and gingerly tried to lift the brown stuff without disturbing the makeup layers underneath. It didn't work. I ended up with a bright spot of white where taupe should have been. Streaks of gray marred my perfect pink blush. There was no recourse but to start all over again.

I cleansed my face with cold cream, dabbed on some skin freshener, applied moisturizer, concealer, foundation, pink blush, two shades of taupe eye shadow, and a thin line of brown eyeliner. Loading my mascara brush with dark brown mascara, I once again—oh so carefully—applied one coat of mascara to both sides of my lashes. Then I slicked on some lipstick, washed down two Tylenol with a cold sip of coffee, and gathered my purse, keys, Bible, and notebook. Finally, I headed out the door.

Since I was running so late, I practically flew my little car to town, careened into the parking lot, and ran lickety-split toward the worship center. Once I hit the foyer, I paused to gather my dignity, straightened my dress, and pasted on my best Sunday-go-to-meetin' smile. Just as the organ prelude ended, I walked circumspectly into the auditorium and found a seat next to my good friends, Mike and Linda. Whew! Was I ever ready for a few quiet moments of spiritual worship.

Halfway through the call to worship I spotted a dear hen friend, Carolanne, standing in the back. She was loaded down with her purse, a box of Sunday school literature, and a Bible big enough to chunk a mule. I motioned for her to join us.

The first hymn began, and since Carolanne wanted to avoid drawing attention to herself, she decided to squeeze into the space at the end of the pew next to Mike. But how could Mike have known what Carolanne was planning to do? He assumed she would want to sit next to the girls—Linda and me. So instead of scooting to his right to make room for her, Mike stood in gentlemanly fashion and stepped out into the aisle.

I could see that Mike and Carolanne were on a collision course and tried in vain to get Mike's attention. The two collided in a most inappropriate manner. Carolanne let out a big whoop and whirled around. Mike grabbed her arm to steady himself, and for a few moments it looked like they were dancing in the Baptist church and, of all things, to the tune of "What a Friend We Have in Jesus."

"Oh, 'scuse me," Mike muttered as he sat down and started to make room for Carolanne where he now thought she wanted to sit—near the end of the pew. But, by this time, Carolanne had changed her mind. I don't know what possessed her to enter the pew facing the three of us. While still clutching the armload of books, she stepped across Mike's knees at the precise moment he started to scoot over. I don't think I've ever seen a woman in such an awkward position, especially in church. There was no way she could have prevented what happened next.

Carolanne dropped that box of Sunday school literature right on Mike's lap. He let out a low groan that caused all eight members of the Mayo family seated in front of us to turn and gaze. Carolanne tried to retrieve her box, but Mike grabbed it and plopped it beside him while muttering, "Just sit down, over there, please." Then he shook his head and added, "I'm glad I've already had my family."

As Carolanne settled between Linda and me, she kept repeating, "I'm so sorry. I should have sat on the end of the pew."

By this time everybody around us had lost their composure. As we stifled our giggles, the pew shook so hard I thought the bolts anchoring it to the floor would pop loose. As I dabbed my eyes with a tissue, I noticed my mascara was coming off again.

We finally gained control and joined with boisterous enthusiasm on the next hymn. After the last stanza, I peeped over Carolanne's shoulder and asked Linda, "Is Mike OK?" She whispered, "I think he finally caught his breath"—a simple comment that sent us into another round of hysteria.

For the rest of the service, Mike sat straight as a rail with his hands clasped in his lap. But there was a silly grin on his face, and every once in a while, he'd whisper another funny observation that would have the entire pew shaking with laughter again.

At the end of the service I could not recall one thing I'd heard from the sermon and yet, strangely, I felt so good inside. Throughout the day and into the next week the flush of joy remained in my heart. On Monday I ran into Carolanne in the grocery store and we laughed one more time. On Friday Linda told me Carolanne had sent Mike a get well card.

Sometimes I wonder, *What's church all about if it's not about enjoying friends, sharing real moments of genuine laughter, fellowship, singing praises, and caring about each other?* Those are gifts from God that make this chick kneel on both drumsticks and worship.

I have to admit, going to church is worth all the trouble of "putting on my face"—even if I do end up crying (or laughing) it all off again!

The One enthroned in heaven laughs.
Psalm 2:4

Church Bulletin Bloopers
(Author Unknown)

Chicken Nugget

Announcements such as these have graced church bulletins around the country:

This afternoon there will be a meeting in the south and north ends of the church. Children will be baptized at both ends.

Tuesday at 4 p.m. there will be a meeting of the Young Mothers' Club. All those wishing to become "Young Mothers," please meet the minister in his study.

Thursday at 8 p.m. there will be an ice cream social. All ladies giving milk, please come early.

This being Easter Sunday, Mrs. Johnson will come forward and lay an egg on the altar.

On Sunday a special collection will be taken to defray the expenses of the new carpet.
All those wishing to do something on the carpet, please come forward and do so.

CHAPTER 33

Struttin' My Stuff

by Rebecca Barlow Jordan

Classmates called me "String Bean." "You don't eat enough to keep a bird alive!" others said. I have sympathy for compulsive overeaters—but when people accused me of undereating, I took offense.

As a teen, I would often sneak midnight snacks into bed, down chocolate bars, and gobble up chips and dips at all hours. But each time I stepped on the scales, zip. Nothing changed. And when I turned sideways—and stuck out my tongue—I still looked like a zipper. I could have been the "fat-free" poster child—before thin was in. Over time, I began to realize that "slender" was just a nice word for "skinny."

"You could be a model," my friends encouraged me. When Twiggy entered the scene, I felt a little better. But then she was a model. I wasn't.

People always talked about the advantages of being tall and slender. Yes, I *could* reach the top locker in school without standing on tiptoe. Yes, maybe I could have excelled in basketball—if my extra long legs hadn't tangled in knots each time I ran down the court (and at my high school, only the guys had a team). And yes, I could wear anything—if I bought clothes in the children's department and let the hem out eight inches.

But along with the advantages, there were also disadvantages—being able to view the tops of everything. I've read that chickens like to perch on the highest roost possible. But what young chick wants to sing soprano on the top row—smack in the middle of a bunch of roosters? Well, yes, me, too: as a teenager, that is. But not when you are seven and eight years old!

"Rebecca, could you duck down a little?" were words so familiar to me. I would automatically begin silently mouthing them whenever anyone tried to snap a group picture with me in it.

In junior high and high school, I begged Mom to talk to my P.E. instructor. "Can't I *please* wear something different? All the other girls look like fully blossomed swans. But with my toothpick legs? I look like a stork on a diet!" How I hated those P.E. shorts!

My 5'9" frame wasn't the only feature that bothered me. I'm sure I inherited some good characteristics from my dad, but there are two things I wish he'd kept to himself (other than his 6'4" height). One of those inherited things was hair. Daddy had lots of it. Oh, I love my hair—its color and even its thickness—but not the way it multiplies on my arms and legs! I'll never forget a classmate's comment in seventh grade. He took one look at my legs, then at the top of his voice yelled, "Man, do you have *hairy* legs!" That did it! I marched right home after school and insisted Mother give me a razor. That took care of the hair on my legs, but a girl can't shave her arms. Under them? Yes. The downy hairs on my forearms grew so thick that when I got cold, they stood at attention like a crop full of brown hay.

Another "gift" my father handed down the "gene" line was freckles. All my friends took to the sun like chickens to a hen house. They may have waddled out white—but they fairly flew back in with gorgeous, brown tans. One time, at about age ten, I braved the sun—cold turkey. No sunscreen, no oil. I emerged as a barbecued chicken, with two-inch blisters on my shoulders. To this day, my only hope of ever getting that tanned look, is if enough freckles decide to have a party and congregate together until they run into one big brown spot.

As a child and teen, I learned to compensate for my tall, freckled, "plain Jane" appearance—by making plenty of straight As. The nickname changed from "String Bean" to "Brain" ("Bird-brain" came much later), but I didn't mind. I took piano lessons, then voice, and found I had musical talent. At 13, I became a published writer—and proudly read the *High School Anthology of Poetry* that year.

Somewhere between 18 and 40, several significant things happened that helped alter my poor self-image. First, I married my tall sweetheart. Learning to write professionally was a second ego booster. Then, in my thirties, I learned the fine art of camouflage. One of my bolder hen friends suggested I might not want to wear my striped sweater with a floral dress. Another chick-friend taught me how to sit straight and how to gracefully strut like a peacock, wearing its vibrant shades of red, greens, and royal blues. Choosing colors and styles that best suited my hen frame helped me avoid the ones that mirrored a giraffe. I even learned to comb my feathers in a new, more becoming way—one that complemented my oval face. Later, another precious hen introduced me to a new miracle makeup that covered my freckled spots. One day I passed the hall mirror and realized this "skinny, ugly stork" had finally blossomed into a slender swan. I had not only learned to live with my appearance—I'd actually begun to appreciate my looks.

But learning to like my outward appearance was only part of the transformation—and really, a much less important one. Long before my birth, with far more detail than Michelangelo could envision, the Master Artist created a sculpture of the person I was to become. Not just the speckled, fair-skinned, "slender" outer shell. He took care to carve out every detail— inside and out. Behind the scenes, God works tirelessly to complete His masterpiece in each of us. When we squawk about God's artistry, like I often did, the Master Potter replies, "Does the clay say to the Potter, 'What are you making?'" (Isaiah 45:9). What right did I have to argue?

One week, in a small intense gathering of hens and roosters, that truth hit me squarely on the beak. From the conference teacher I heard, "It's not your ability or performance—what you do or don't do. Nor is it your appearance. It's who you are—and who you are becoming in Christ that matters. Because God's love covers a multitude of feathered faults. In His sight, because of God's Son, as His child, you are A+—*perfect*. And when the Creator starts a beautiful work, He always finishes it." Our job? To rest in the Potter's hands.

I had heard similar words from the time I was a speckled chick—when my personal relationship with Jesus Christ really began. But like older hens sometimes do, I had forgotten the very nuggets that fed my body and spirit. This time I ate and drank in those words until I felt full, and—well—like a gorgeous, plumped-up hen.

Now I can honestly say I love this season in my life. I love what I do. I love being tall and "slender"—even though I *can* see the dust on the top of my refrigerator. I even love who I am and who I'm becoming. But more importantly, I love who God is—a marvelous Potter, a patient Father, and a loving Friend.

As I cooperate with God in His shaping of my interior, I'm also still working on the outer shell, trying to heed the words of one of my favorite poets, Robert Browning: "My business is not to remake myself, but make the absolute best of what God made."

The other day I bought contact lenses. For the first time in years, I could actually see my eyebrows! But I also saw other things—wrinkles, adult freckles (now called "liver spots"), and gray hairs that seemed to grow up overnight. The glasses I had worn for several years, just like God's selective vision, had hidden those tiny flaws from my eyes. But what really blew my feathers off was my recent yearly checkup.

The nurse measured my full height while I stood barefoot against the wall. "Five feet nine and three quarter inches," she crowed.

"Impossible," I said. "Don't people start shrinking at midlife?" For years, my husband has been telling me I'm blossoming. Nevertheless, a few of my blossomin' petals wilted as I left the doctor's office that day. As I grew older, I had planned on growing out—not on continuing to grow up.

Then another thought hit me like a 20-pound sack of feed. Confidently, I stretched my neck and smiled. *God sees me as perfect.* As I strutted out the door, I felt ten feet tall—and proud of every inch!

For you created my inmost being;
you knit me together in my mother's womb.
I praise you because I am fearfully
and wonderfully made.
Psalm 139:13-14

Chicken Nugget

Author's Paraphrase of First Corinthians 13:11

When I was a chick,
I talked like a chick,
I thought like a chick,
I reasoned like a chick.
But when I became a hen,
I put chickie ways behind me.

SECTION V

I Think I Shell!

Confidence in Exercising Gifts and Talents

CHAPTER 34

Grins in the Hen Pen

by Becky Freeman

"Are you hungry?" I asked my new friend, Annette, as we headed toward the lunch counter.

"I don't know," Annette confessed. "I've been so nervous about meeting you, you being a famous author and all."

"Oh, Annette," I laughed aloud, "in my hometown, I'm nobody. Just plain ol' Becky."

"You don't get recognized wherever you go?"

"Yes, I do get recognized—as Zach, Zeke, Rachel, or Gabe's mom. Or sometimes as 'that crazy lady who's always forgetting her keys and sunglasses.' Believe me, nobody thinks what I do is a big deal in Greenville, Texas."

With that we took our trays and went through the food line, picking out soup, salad, and yummy desserts. Then we made our way to a table in a room adorned with cute country knickknacks and breathed in the wonderful aromas of apple-spice potpourri, chocolate truffles, and hazelnut coffee.

After offering a quick blessing, I opened my eyes and noticed a nicely dressed woman standing beside our table.

"Excuse me," she said, "but are you Becky Freeman? The one who writes those funny books?"

I stole an awkward glance at Annette and whispered. "This never happens. Really, Annette. I'm nobody." Then I turned to the lady and answered, "Well, yes, I'm the one."

"Oh, oh, oh!" she gushed, "you have no idea. You have *no* idea what your books have meant to me." At this point she began to cry, struggling to get the words out. She reached in her purse for a tissue. "I'm so embarrassed. I don't ever do this. I'm normally not this emotional. But I've had a tough year, and I just had to come over and thank you for ma—making me, ma-making me—laugh."

I thanked her for coming over, telling her how much her encouragement meant. The woman walked away, dabbing at her eyes and smiling through her tears.

Annette winked as she placed her napkin in her lap. "Well, Becky Nobody, that was interesting."

"Honest," I answered with a laugh, "this has never happened before! So OK. Every now and then, I'm a little bit of a Somebody."

"How does it make you feel to know you've impacted someone's life like that?"

"All I can tell you, Annette, is this is what makes writing worth all the effort. To make people smile—to offer even a small break of laughter when life closes in, is a blessing that's hard to describe."

Making a career out of laughter has turned out to be the greatest surprise of my third decade. As my mother is fond of saying, "Who'd have thunked it?" I certainly didn't start out, as a child, dreaming of the day I would grow up to be laughed at. On the contrary, I was often shy and withdrawn. At school, I felt much like the invisible girl.

But God has this wonderful sense of humor. With the advent of puberty, my peculiar personality began to bloom—

the kind of personality that could either make a parent run screaming in frustration or fall into a fit of hilarity. Thankfully, God gave me the gift of a laughing family. Destined to go through teenagehood (and what appears to be the rest of my mortal life) making lots of mistakes, God, in His great mercy, has at least allowed me to be entertaining while I'm at it.

So it is with no small amount of pride that I say, "I come from a long line of nuts." As I've noted, the folks in our family tree generally embrace a "what-could-be-funny-about-this" view of life. They have what I call "Erma Eyes," after my heroine of humor, the late Erma Bombeck.

I once received a card from Erma Bombeck in response to a letter of admiration and concern I'd sent her. The card sits in a small gold frame above my writing desk and reads,

"Dear Becky, I cannot begin to tell you how much your kind letter meant to me. I am doing well and am ready to start writing yet another book. As George Burns once said, 'I can't die. I'm booked.' It is the outpouring of concern from letters like yours that keeps me going. Thanks again, I am so appreciative. I would love to see your new book! Love, Erma."

I wonder how many of us whom Erma made laugh over the years, also shed tears on the day she died? What admiring reader didn't feel, after reading a Bombeck column or book, that they must be somehow related to her crazy family? One of my favorite Erma stories occurred when her children asked where socks went when they disappeared. In classic Erma style, she answered, "They go to be with Jesus." I can't help but wonder if Jesus greeted Erma at heaven's gate with a welcoming embrace of laughter—and a basket filled with socks.

For truly humor is a gift from above, and I think one of heaven's greatest surprises will be the laughter of Christ ringing through eternity. Solomon once described a merry heart as a healing balm. And how true that statement has proven to be. Scientists now tell us that laughter relaxes our bodies; takes the sting out of pain; provides relief from fear, worry, and stress; and can even prolong life.

The best part of writing this book has been the laughter that has erupted among us "Hens with Pens"—often through tears or times of great stress. As we chicks near the end of this writing project, all of us are experiencing some level of mental fatigue. Gracie called this morning, and we chatted about our failing minds. "I think what's happened," I explained, "is that in the process of writing this book, we've all used up our given quota of brain cells. To finish the book, we are going to have to put our few remaining brain cells together and just hope and pray we come up with enough neurons to add up to one whole brain." She laughed. I laughed. And soon we were ready to tackle our waiting assignments with renewed perspective.

Nothing frees creativity like laughter. As a matter of fact, a test was done at the University of Maryland where they took a group of people and let them watch five minutes of television bloopers. At the same time another group was treated to five minutes of a video about mathematics entitled, "The Area Under a Curve." (Now doesn't that title just grab you?) After the videos, both groups were given a series of problems to solve. Results? The group that had been laughing over the bloopers were 300 to 500 percent more likely to come up with creative, successful solutions to the problems than their geometrically bored counterparts.

Someday, I think, scientists will discover that a new brain cell pops into existence with every chuckle we take. Look at all the learning kids do early in life! Perhaps it is because they laugh 400 times a day compared to an adult's average: a mere dozen daily chuckles.

To enjoy humor, to view the world through "Erma Eyes," to share the gift of laughter with someone else—what wonderful ways to live our days! "So long as there's a bit of a laugh going," wrote D. H. Lawrence, "things are all right." So many of the people we've loved and admired throughout history have a wonderful combination of wisdom, sprinkled with the confetti of mirth. In his book, *Surprised by Laughter*, Dr. Terry Lindvall wrote of C. S. Lewis, "One bright and compelling feature we can see, sparkling in his sunlight and dancing in his moonlight, is laughter." But did you know Lewis had a mentor in humor? He was the oft-quoted English commentator, G. K. Chesterson. Lindvall writes, "[Chesterson] was a cheerleader for truth, goodness, and the humorous ways of God. He entered Lewis' life as a kindly and gallant guardian angel, a giant, laughing cherub." Laughter is, in truth, quite contagious.

This weekend I spoke at a women's conference, and the woman introducing me became tongue-tied and ended up accidentally pronouncing my name "Frecky Beeman." I loved it! My laughter spawned a round of more infectious laughter. The name stuck all weekend, and I'm thinking about adopting it permanently. I have a friend whose real, given name is Win Shields. Win loves his name because he makes people smile whenever he gives it out. How much fun it would be to have a name that would say to the world, "Go ahead, enjoy a laugh on me."

So call me Becky or call me Frecky. It's all the same to me.

As long as you smile when you say it.

He that is of a merry heart hath a continual feast.
Proverbs 15:15 KJV

How "The Hens with Pens" Would Answer the Question:

Chicken Nugget

Why did the chicken cross the road?

Practical, "Get-real" Gracie Hen: A slick chick couldn't waste time meandering around the countryside; she was ready to cross that road off her "to-do" list. (And I think she had a cute little rooster waiting for her on the other side.)

Soft-spoken, Thoughtful Fran Hen: She was so happy that she decided to share her joy by visiting her neighbors across the street. She'd heard they were in need, so she brought them a basket of eggs.

All-out-for-God Suzie Hen: I think that chicken had a calling from God on her life. She was just sitting around laying eggs listening to some praise music when God told her to go cluck for Jesus, and off she went to minister to hurting chicks in the barnyard.

Prayerful, Cautious Rebecca Hen: Do we know the chicken really ever crossed the road? Did she walk straight across the road or did she veer a little to the left? We have to think these things through, gals. I'd like to pray about it.

Bewildered and Amusing Becky Hen: She was wandering around, trying to remember where she'd laid her car keys, sunglasses, and her last dozen eggs.

CHAPTER 35

Keep Pecking and Scratching

by Fran Caffey Sandin

"You may think you're smart because you graduated valedictorian in your little high school class of 23," Miss Franke retorted briskly, "but don't think you can make it through *this* nursing program. It is much too hard."

As I sat across the desk from this big white leghorn hen, I felt my face begin to flush. How dare she dash my dreams! I had wanted to be a nurse since I was six years old, and this was the only school we could afford. My mother and dad sat beside me. After listening to her adamant comments, we just looked at each other. We were puzzled, not expecting such a harsh initiation into college life. In my naiveté, I thought she would be delighted to see me. Now I was getting angry.

"Miss Franke, all I need is a chance," I began to plead. "I'm a hard worker. I know I can make it."

"Well, we'll see," she said disparagingly. "If you decide to start, here are some papers to fill out." She shoved the papers toward me.

Soon we were in the hallway, having been escorted out of the office. As I stood there with the papers in my hand, I gritted my teeth and thought, *I'll show you. I'll show you!*

Looking back, I wonder if Miss Franke was really a psychologist. Maybe she knew all along that this East Texas farm girl needed an extra motivational push when the times got tough. For the next four years, including summers, I worked and studied. At times, I did feel like quitting. But when a sinking spell would come, I'd remember Miss Franke, and anger would rise up in my chicken heart. Then I'd strut my feathers and cluck, "I'll show you!"

I signed up for all the extra help classes (especially for physics and organic chemistry) and worked like a little red hen with my beak to the grindstone. My family uplifted and prayed for me. Finally, after many classmates had dropped out, the ones of us who persevered reached our goal. Having Miss Franke at my graduation was the ultimate joy. She even smiled. *Boy, did I show her!*

I never dreamed, at that graduation moment, that I'd be attending a writer's conference in the future. I'll never forget the words of the keynote speaker, "The definition of an author is a writer who did not quit." I had no big aspirations to become a writer, but I felt compelled to share a story from my life's experience. I simply wanted to help other parents who, like me, had experienced the loss of a child.

It took four years to write the first draft of my book, *See You Later, Jeffrey.* Once I finished typing the last page, I had no idea what to do next. So I went to the public library and checked out books on "How to Submit a Manuscript." Looking back, I realize my first attempts weren't all that great, but people encouraged me along the way. I began sending out my story—and it boomeranged back. Rejection, rejection, rejection. It would have been so easy to give up. In fact, the manuscript lay in my desk drawer for months at a time because I didn't know what my next step should be.

Rejects were painful, as everyone knows. So I learned to call them "returns" instead of rejection. That sounded so much better. After 20 returns, I decided I needed some help. So through a friend's mother, who was also an author, I learned of an upcoming writer's conference.

As a result of attending the conference, I found the courage to submit two magazine articles, both of which were published while I was still revising the book manuscript. The following year, I attended the conference again and took the reworked manuscript, my 27th submission. To my delight, the editor representing a large publishing house took the manuscript. A few months later I received a contract, and the following year, the book was published—11 years after I had first begun to write.

Sometimes it is hard to hang in there, to keep on pecking and scratching. Many times after we've felt God leading us into a task beyond our natural ability, we have to deal with rejections. While waiting, we may spend time in some kind of wilderness or get delayed dealing with family stresses. But in the midst of our humbling experiences, we come to recognize that all our talents are from our Creator. When He calls us to a task, He provides the supernatural strength and the wisdom to see us through. He faithfully does His part. We just need to do ours—and keep on pecking, scratching, and persevering for His glory.

And let us not lose heart in doing good, for in due time we
shall reap if we do not grow weary.
Galatians 6:9 NASB

Chicken Nugget

The 7 Habits of Highly Effective Hens

1. Pray—Seek God's direction. Define your purpose for wanting to be involved in the endeavor.

2. Principles—Set high standards and determine not to compromise, no matter what.

3. Preparation—Be willing to pay the price to become a professional. Keep learning.

4. Power—Rely upon the Holy Spirit's supernatural power to lend support and wisdom.

5. Patience—Wait on God's timing. He loves you and He knows best.

6. Politeness—Kindness is of utmost importance in interpersonal communications.

7. Praise—Keep a personal time alone with God. Seek to please Him and not exalt self.

CHAPTER 36

From the Beaks of Babes

by Gracie Malone

Our son, Mike, walked through the front door and greeted his toddler, Montana, with a hearty, "Hi!"

Montana grinned, nodded his head, and declared himself, "Fine!" Our little grandson, before he was even two, had already mastered a grown-up shortcut to real communication—the pat answer. Sometimes we all lapse into the conversational mode of "auto-talk" and find we haven't really communicated at all.

The other day, I was clipping through the mall when I spotted an old friend. I greeted her as I whizzed by, "How are you?"

"Just fine!" she answered as she darted into the health food store. Later I wondered how she really was, and thought, *I could have slowed my pace a bit.* But she was in a hurry too, and who's got time to talk?

Unfortunately, many of our adult conversations consist of two or three words uttered on the run. We nod, grin, grunt, quip, or wave, and just keep-a-goin'. It's cute when a toddler like Montana parrots a greeting, but it's not so cute when grown-up conversations remain on the automatic-response level.

Our chicks were barely sprouting pinions when my husband, Joe, and I realized the importance of connecting with our brood. Later on as they became teenagers we looked for opportunities to have more than a passing "Hi, how are you doing" conversation.

After work, Joe often wrestled with the boys in their room or helped them with projects. I tended the flower beds as they played outside or shot hoops in the driveway. I watched my teens polish their cars and learned to "hang out" with them in our family room.

Meaningful moments occurred at odd times and in unexpected places.

One evening while watching TV, Jason, our impulsive high-schooler, abruptly announced, "I'm hungry for tacos," hinting he wanted to make the famous fast-food "run for the border." My first reaction was typically parental—it was after ten and he'd skipped supper. But instead of pointing this out, I decided to cultivate our friendship.

Noting Jason's bare feet, I suggested, "How 'bout I drive?"

In the car Jason relaxed and chatted all the way to town. Waiting our turn at the take-out window, he even discussed his girlfriend problems. Conversation flowed freely as I fumbled through my purse, until I turned on the light to count change. Abruptly, he slid down in his seat and shrieked, "Mom, somebody might see me with you!" Then he grinned playfully as he explained, "Hey, being out with your mother at night is definitely not cool."

Today when our chickens come home to roost, I still try to be available and watch for listening opportunities. Recently I helped our adult son, Matt, rake leaves in the yard. As I held the bags open for him, he talked about his kids and his new position at work. (And, I might add, he didn't even duck behind a bush when the neighbors drove by.)

As I interact with my brood, I remember the words of James 1:19: "Be quick to listen, slow to speak." Communication experts agree, claiming we should listen 70 percent of the time and speak only 30 percent of the time. Being a wise old hen makes it hard for me to stop squawking, but it's amazing what I've learned by keeping my beak shut.

One day after school Jason revealed that a classmate had brought pornographic videos to school—to sell! I stifled a reaction until I heard more vital information, "Mom, he thinks he's homosexual." By listening and not reacting, a whole range of issues we needed to discuss were opened up.

Also through the years I've realized the importance of expressing emotion to effectively communicate with our children. Instead of offering platitudes such as, "Don't be angry . . . don't feel badly . . . don't cry," I encourage them to talk about their emotions by asking questions: "How did that affect you?" or "What did you feel?" Once the feelings are exposed, I can identify and work on the underlying causes of our offspring's pain. Like ironing wrinkles out of a starched shirt, I can help smooth our chicks' ruffled feathers with encouraging words.

As our family has learned to communicate on a deeper level, all sorts of issues have been up for discussion—including some mistakes Joe and I have made. It isn't easy to "fess up" when we've erred, but to cover up or deny our part of a problem would not only set a poor example, it would lead to communication breakdown. Joe and I try to model the biblical way of dealing with failure by admitting we were wrong and saying we're sorry.

Even when it's difficult to do, we know we are opening the door for better two-way communication.

Often "speaking the truth in love" (Ephesians 4:15) has taught us a better way to offer advice or confront one of our brood. If there's "fowl play" and one of our chicks gets in trouble, we gather our brood and prayerfully run for shelter under God's wings. Joe and I consider our home a refuge, a coop where every chicken feels safe and comfortable.

Alongside Grandma's favorite recipes we serve hearty portions of food for the soul including double helpings of respect and love.

Understanding our differences in temperament and respecting our individual opinions helps keep the communication lines open too. Every fowl in our henhouse is unique.

Jason, like me, flocks to people. Matt and Mike, our oldest two, are computer wizards like their dad. Matt's wife, Rebecca, is an up-front, bold, flight attendant who spends her free hours devouring the classics. Mike's wife, Jeanna, a classy hairdresser, is an easygoing, fun-loving chick who dotes on her family. When the guys spew computereeze or the gals flutter over an issue, I'm usually the one filling in the communication gaps. I guess you could say I'm the official family go-between gap-gabber.

Our grandkids also have distinct personalities, and their own individual communication styles. One Christmas we saw their unique temperaments emerge as we decorated a gumdrop tree. Luke wanted matching colors on every branch. Connor turned melancholy because Luke was "bossy and takes too long." Sunny little Mary Catherine giggled and ate gumdrops, while easygoing Montana nonchalantly observed. Through many years of interaction we've remained a close knit family. Our "eggstra" special relationship has come, in part, because of communicating.

One morning our three-year-old grandson Connor handed the telephone to his mother. "Call Grandma Gracie," he pleaded, "I have soooo many things to say to her."

Rebecca dialed the number, then Connor took over. When I answered I heard him say, "It's me!"

I was thrilled to hear his little voice. Connor didn't call to share earth-shattering news that day but just to chat. Looks like we've got another lets-talk-it-over Malone verbalizing his way up the branches of our noisy family tree.

Like apples of gold in settings of silver
is a word spoken in right circumstances.
Proverbs 25:11 NASB

Chicken Nugget

Scrambled Eggs

Sometimes we try too hard to make a point and end up making no sense at all. These are some of my favorite real-life mixed metaphors, used by public officials, from the book, Anguished English.

The sacred cows have come home
to roost with a vengeance.

I wouldn't be caught dead in that movie
with a ten foot pole.

That snake in the grass is barking up the wrong tree.

These hemorrhoids are a real pain in the neck.

It's as easy as falling off a piece of cake.

From now on, I'm watching everything you do
with a fine-tuned comb.

CHAPTER 37

Stretchin' My Wings

by Rebecca Barlow Jordan

It started out as an innocent attraction. But as the years passed, it turned into a full-fledged love affair.

I can't remember exactly when I first fell in love with words. But as a child and teen, summer after summer I sat enthralled in my fantasy world—and read tales born out of the lives of ordinary characters, with consonants and vowels woven skillfully together with pluck and persistence. By whom? Writers. Writers opened to me worlds of mystery, romance, inspiration, poetry, fiction, and biographies. I loved them all. Each written page was an art, a sculpture of experiences and moods, of lives, and of truthful lessons. Each book was a creative treasure of someone's imagination or divine inspiration.

I soon found that words could either be used as a curse— or as a gift of encouragement. "There is enough ugliness in the world," I'd say. "I want to write about beauty. I want to inspire." I started with greeting cards. When others asked me to describe my work, sometimes I'd reply, "I'm a 'Band-Aid' dispenser." Greeting cards are like Band-Aids. They temporarily comfort the hurts with laughter or consolation until permanent healing occurs.

Several years later, when editors asked, "Would you be willing to try something new?" each time I gulped and said, "Sure." But afterwards I'd moan, "I've never done this before—I can't do it!" And then God would gently remind me that the same gift that penned a poem or devotional could also encourage others through articles, calendars, stories, newspaper columns— whatever He wanted me to do. So I tried. Some projects took longer. They didn't just roll off my pen and drop onto the paper like polished diamonds of ink.

Soon I discovered this gift of words is not always what it seems "cracked" up to be. I had visualized that the co-writing of my first book, *Marriage Toners*, with my husband, Larry, would be such a romantic experience. He and I would escape to a borrowed lake house, recount our blessings, and dispense great doses of marital encouragement to others. That particular getaway experience did bring us even closer together, but not in the way I expected. Working on the project reemphasized our unique differences—giving us ample opportunities to practice our own advice to others. Not only that, Larry's father died the week preceding our "writing retreat." It was with much sweat and tears that we completed the bulk of our manuscript during that next week at the lake house.

There were times when I wanted to quit, or at least surrender the verbal gift of words—times when it was safer to communicate with only my pen, not my beak. That's the way I was feeling some time ago when I was visiting Jane, a depressed and suicidal woman.

After hearing me try to convince her that life was indeed worth living, Jane had thanked me repeatedly for our divine encounter that night. Then, a few months later, I stopped by to see her again. This time (apparently in her eyes), I had changed from an angel of mercy to an attacking enemy—all because of three words I uttered in haste.

For 30 minutes I had listened to Jane spew out criticism of her husband, children, and God Himself. Then I made a blunt accusation: "You are bitter."

"Get out of my *house—now!*" she yelled. "I didn't invite you here, and you have no right to speak to me that way!"

Later, God allowed me to see how I had failed in my knee-jerk response to that delicate situation. Instead of listening to a hurting woman bare her pain, I poured salty words into her open wounds. I had not yet earned the right to reprove her. With my careless words, I judged a woman I hardly knew.

At other times, my words brought misunderstanding. On Sunday mornings, in what we called the "Crows-nest" class (the balcony), I taught our church's two hearing-impaired women. One Sunday morning the Bible passage told how Paul had admonished two fighting women to reconcile. As their deaf interpreter, I didn't realize at the time that the two women were jealous of each other. After class, one of them refused to "talk" to me.

Later, over coffee, with our fingers flying through the air, we resolved the situation. In class she mistakenly thought I had been pointing a finger at her personally, not simply talking about a biblical character.

Wanting to try new ways to use this gift of words, I eventually ventured into public speaking. For more than 20 years I had taught various ages in our church. But repeatedly I had avoided any formal training in public speaking and had done very little solo "speaking." I had nightmares of snoring audiences, mental blank-outs, forgetting my notes, and stage fright. I did buy one popular speaker's training course—on tape—and listened to it no less than 10 times over a period of years. Finally, one day, I surrendered with, "OK, God, if you want me to speak, I'll do it." I made a list of 10 topics and absentmindedly shoved it into my memory drawer. But God didn't forget. The next week, the phone rang.

"Rebecca," a lady's pleasant voice asked, "would you come and speak to our ladies' luncheon next month? You can choose the topic."

I started to object, but instead said, "Yes, I'd love to."

A few weeks passed. One morning I was reading my Bible and ran across two words. I read them again: "Jesus taught." Some people even called Him, "Good Teacher." I flipped pages and kept finding the same words. Nowhere did I see, "Jesus was a speaker."

Yes! A matter of semantics, I thought. Speaking is just like teaching. My "wings" of confidence began to grow.

I try to remember God's whispers of encouragement when I'm speaking and my worst nightmare does happen—like the time I forgot my memorized "intro" speech at a writer's conference. "Words can change your life," I challenged the conferees, "like the words I found in my grandmother's Bible. Those words are. . . ." I paused. "They are. . . ." I hesitated again, searching for the memory "seed" scattered somewhere in my birdbrain.

Flustered, I blurted out, "I can't remember the words, but they are changing my life." A ripple of laughter eased the moment and another fellow speaker saved the day: "Go to her class—you'll find out how to change your life there."

Maybe it was that accidental incident that challenged me to loosen my serious feathers a bit. But a few days later I was browsing through my library for some helps on humor and ran across an antiquated book on writing. The author's words were not encouraging: "I do not believe that it is possible for anyone to learn to be humorous. . . . The writing of humor is an art by itself. Very few possess the ability. . . . Do not try to be funny, if you are not naturally humorous. Bad narrative or argument is bad enough, but bad humor is an abomination."

To further fuel my lack of confidence, I still remembered my own husband's advice a few years ago: "Honey, you're either funny, or you're not funny. And honey, you're not funny." Like a train without a caboose, my jokes were often abandoned without a punch line.

God must have purposefully planned my next writing project to include—you guessed it—some humor. So I reluctantly agreed to try a little light tickling with my own feathered pen. A few chuckles later, my husband has become my best cheerleader.

"I can't be funny," I sigh.

"Yes, you can—with God's help," he answers. So God continues to stretch and tickle my wings.

I've discovered that writing humor is a lot like dispensing Band-Aids. Laughter covers the hurt until permanent healing comes—and often makes the truth more manageable.

Whether we're soothing ruffled feathers (including our own), encouraging wet hens, or tickling someone's chicken bone, the gift of words is truly that—a gift from God to use wisely. At one of our hen meetings, Becky once laughed and said, "I guess we all have goosebumps underneath our hen feathers." She was right. But wherever this gift of words leads—even if it's outside my "comfort coop," it helps me to remember that with God, all things are possible. (I've even learned to tell a whole, complete joke—caboose and all.)

To love what you do and feel that it matters—well, there's nothing like it. And when I'm writing, speaking—or even signing—the Father's words, it's a joy to know that my work with words truly does matter.

Work? Yes. But sometimes, using this gift of words is so much fun, I almost feel guilty getting paid for it.

But don't tell that to my editor.

The tongue of the wise brings healing.
Proverbs 12:18

Rebecca's Writing Rules of Disorder

1. Break all the rules—at least once.
2. Think about the subjects you know. Then write about something you don't know.
3. Write it—and they will buy it. (They sure won't if you don't.)
4. Follow all the rules—at least once.
5. Let your best friends and family read your stuff. Then do the opposite of what they say.
6. Go ahead and give up. Then try again tomorrow.
7. Never take an editor's word as the last word (regarding rejection, that is).
8. Instead of selling 50 percent of what you write, sell 100 percent of what you don't write. (Query, query, query.)
9. Never trust anything mechanical.
10. Flattering the editors will get you nowhere. Good manuscripts might make it to their desk.

"There is no limit to what God can do with a man, providing he will not touch the glory."
—Author Unknown (from my grandmother's Bible)

CHAPTER 38

Squawkin' and Talkin'

by Becky Freeman

I dialed the number and put the receiver to my ear, grateful for the cheerful, matter-of-fact voice saying "Hello" on the other end. It was my Gracie, our own Henny Penny. (I don't know why I call her "my Gracie"—she belongs to lots of folks. I only use "my" in front of relative's names: my mother, my Aunt Etta, my Nonnie, my sister. I guess Gracie is somewhere between a friend and all of the above.)

"Gracie!" I squawked. "Help! I just said 'yes' to giving a talk at a luncheon. You've done lots of them, so I need to know everything there is to know about public speaking. Would you believe people think just because I can write, I can talk, too! In front of big groups, no less!"

"Hon, it'll be fine," Gracie soothed. "Tell you what—I was about to call you for some help with an article I'm working on. How about you help me with that, and I'll give you a few pointers for your talk? You wanna meet me at Taco Bueno at, say, 11:30?"

"OK. Yes. Taco Bueno. In twenty minutes. You, me, nachos, and everything we both know about speaking and writing—"

"Which could probably fit on one taco chip," Gracie quipped.

Within a half an hour, Gracie and I were sitting in a booth, talkin' turkey and eatin' tacos. After I helped tweak her article with additional humor (my standard contribution), she handed me a copy of Carol Kent's book, *Speak Up With Confidence*, and an outline from Florence Littauer's CLASS seminar.

"Now Becky, it is really very simple. You just make an outline with an introduction, three points, and a conclusion. Then under each point tell an illustration, an example, and any resources you might have."

I went home and began my outline. Then I recorded and re-recorded my talk until I'd listened to myself about 187 times. I was so tired of my own voice, I thought I'd slap myself if I said another word. I was beyond prepared. What I longed for now was a live audience to take the place of my all-too-familiar reflection in the mirror.

My initial experiences in speaking were basically positive and encouraging. I mostly came away feeling enormously relieved and awed that God could actually use my words, verbally speaking, to encourage others. But the strangest pattern began to emerge later.

Inevitably, something embarrassing would happen—the sort of thing that would probably "undo" a normal person, but I, being me, found them oddly funny.

The first time I ever spoke—for a Christmas Coffee—I inadvertently leaned against a votive candle and caught my hair on fire. (Imagine the fragrance that filled the room. It wasn't cinnamon potpourri!)

The next time I spoke at a Mother's Day luncheon. Just before I got up, my mother pointed to the front of my white blouse. During lunch I'd unknowingly leaned against the tip of an open black marker sticking out of my book. I looked as though some creative toddler had been using my front as an art pad.

Twice I have gone to the platform, only to have buttons pop off my dress before I was halfway through my introduction.

Once, I thought I'd made it through the *perfect* speaking event—unscathed by scandal. You could feel God's presence in the room that evening. There was riotous laughter and tender tears; hearts were encouraged and changed. Then, just as I was waving good-bye to the pastor, music minister, and their wives, I fell straight back off of a step on my backside. During the fall, my dress slid, very unchurch, unladylike, half way up my thighs. The really sad thing was, it didn't hurt because apparently I have so much padding behind me, I simply bounced. The next day, only my pride was sore.

Today I can honestly say that I *love* speaking, in spite of the occasional setbacks and scenes of humiliation. I've found most anything can be turned into an occasion for laughter. I've finally relaxed enough to just be myself, and I've realized the power of sharing short stories that illustrate deeper spiritual truths.

But before the current Thrill of Oratory, I experienced the ultimate Agony of De Feet (in De Mouth). Early on, shortly after the debut of *Worms in My Tea*, I had my first painful public speaking experience. Only now, after four years, am I able to share it without deep twinges of pain.

I spoke to Southern Baptist librarians on the topic, "God Uses Peculiar People." I was extremely well-received; I loved them, and they loved me right back! My husband was there, beaming with pride. He and I fairly floated back to the hotel. The evaluations, more than 100 of them, came back with glowing words of praise for my keynote's contribution to the week-long event.

But any shred of pride that might have crept in my heart was about to be scrambled into egg on my face.

The following morning, Scott drove me to another section of the city to speak at another event. The crowd was small, the women appeared to be well-to-do, the church old and elegant. Still, I gave the same fun talk about how God enjoys peculiar people, sometimes putting them in odd circumstances and using them for His glory. But the response was not the same. In fact, the woman who had booked me was strangely quiet afterwards.

When I returned home to Texas, I received a letter in the mail from the second event coordinator unpreceded by any warning, no personal phone call, nothing to soften the blow. It said, in no uncertain terms, that the event went well except for one thing: I had been a huge disappointment. My talk was "shallow," and I was obviously an unseasoned unprofessional. Just to drive the point home where it was sure to hurt—they asked for half of their money back.

Still reeling, but realizing I had to share what had happened with my agent, I phoned him. He was kind, apologetic, and understanding and, he added reluctantly, a copy of the angry letter had already landed on his desk. I was soon to discover that this woman also sent a copy to my publisher's publicist who had, out of the goodness of her heart, acted as an unpaid go-between for this one event.

I wanted to die with the pain. It was a physical wrenching deep in my gut. For days, even weeks afterwards, if I let my mind slip down the painful path, I'd find myself drenched in tears all over again.

How could I have given the exact same talk to a crowd the night before where women were overcome with joy as they stood in line, some with tears in their eyes, to shake my hand in gratitude and then be told I was a complete failure and "spiritually shallow" the very next morning.

Everything human inside me wanted to scream and lash out. I wrote a first draft of a letter giving those "high and mighty bluebloods" a piece of my mind (which I really could not afford to lose). Eventually, I swallowed my pride, decided to take the high road instead, tore up the paper, wrote a simple, gracious letter enclosing the entire fee they had paid me—a fee our family had counted on to get us through the next few weeks of bills. I never heard another peep from them. (Though I must say they didn't waste any time in depositing the check!)

How would I ever get back in front of a group after this? How had I ever dared to think I'd been gifted by God to share my puny little stories? I was not only becoming yellow and more chicken each day, I wanted to curl up in my eggshell and never peck myself out again. Certainly not in front of a crowd.

Looking back I can see what happened, and I'm ever grateful it happened early on rather than later on. Clearly God was showing me that I must speak out of obedience to Him and not for the approval of man. All applause and praise belongs to Him, and though I can learn and grow from my mistakes, rejection is not something I need to absorb. I can lay the burden of rejection on my Savior's shoulders, too. My job is to give Him glory in all that I do—washing dishes, wiping noses, writing, and speaking. Period.

During what I call my "recovery" period, I went to Carol Kent's "Speak Up With Confidence" course. I loved the sound of that—speak up, with confidence! Over the coming months

Carol and I would become good friends. She helped me see my strengths again and became a source of abiding encouragement. But perhaps the best gift Carol ever gave me was inviting me to lunch and then back to her hotel room where we put our feet up and just visited. When I found the courage to confess what had happened to me, she stopped, looked at me with eyes full of compassion and said, "Oh, Becky, if only you'd called. I've had similar painful experiences."

"*You?*" I asked, finding it hard to believe that this incredible woman could have ever been harshly critiqued.

"Oh, yes!" Then she shared a couple of horror stories that strangely made me feel oh-so-much better. Even Liz Higgs, who is one of the best and funniest speakers around, talks about what she calls her "Ishtar" moment—when one of her talks to her fellow speaking peers landed with a dull thud. But she got up again the following year—and received a standing ovation. She's since become one of the few people to receive the highest honor bestowed by the National Speaking Association.

I believe that God, in His farseeing mercy, often humbles us early in our ministries so that we determine, from the get-go, just who it is we are working for. An audience? Our own fulfillment? Or is it out of obedience to the One who has given us something to say?

Some of you reading this may feel God asking you to speak up for Him. I want to make it clear that I believe in the value of good training, and even more in the value of mentoring.

But the best advice I could give you as you step out of the nest and begin to follow His leading comes from the apostle Paul: "Do your work heartily, as to the Lord, rather than for men."

It is God, and God alone, who turns our chicken squawking into words of blessing.

So we speak, not as pleasing men, but God, who
examines our hearts.
1 Thessalonians 2:4 NASB

Six Steps to Hatching a Great Story

Chicken Nugget

1. Pick a personal story—something dramatic, funny, interesting or tragic that has happened to you.
2. Write it down, then edit it to one page, typewritten, and double spaced. You should be able to tell it in less than two minutes.
3. Build suspense. Don't give away information too soon. You might say things like, "I thought this would be a day like any other. I was wrong," or "I woke up and asked myself, 'What's wrong with me?'"
4. Don't tell people what you are going to tell them. Just jump right in to your talk with something like, "I was nine years old and I saw my father walking up a ladder into the attic. . . ."
5. Use accents, variation of voice, wide body gestures, and facial expression to keep the audience on its toes. Be generous with word pictures so they can visualize what you are saying.
6. Don't forget the Power of the Pause. Pauses are as important as talking.

CHAPTER 39

Chicken Feed

by Gracie Malone

In preparation to teach a class of teenage chicks in Sunday school, I studied the Bible daily and came to class with pages of notes and visual aids tucked under my wing; but even though I taught fervently, I wasn't getting through to those feisty pullets. For several weeks my brood huddled in a circle looking bored while I attempted to impart a spiritual truth that was way over my own head. Sunday after Sunday I waddled out of my classroom with the uneasy feeling that I just laid another Grade AA extra large egg!

I was about ready to throw in the egg basket, when one Sunday morning I finally witnessed a burst of enthusiasm from one of my chickens. The experience was an event that literally changed the course of my life. Right in the middle of the lesson, this young lady fluttered to the edge of her chair, sucked in a big gulp of air, and started flapping her wings. My little chicken heart beat wildly as I tried to recall what I'd just said to impress her so. But then, she pointed one sharp talon at her friend on the other side of the circle, opened her beak wide and squawked, "Where did you get those shoes? If those are not the cutest things I've ever seen!" My feathers fell. I practically limped out of the class, laden with discouragement.

After a full week of soul-searching, I resigned as a teacher and joined a class for women where I could be mentored by an older hen friend, Johanna. I wanted to teach like Johanna, but obviously I needed help. The mentoring relationship that developed between us provided a much-needed boost to my sagging self-confidence. Even though I still remember some of the deep truths Johanna taught, I learned even more by following her example. I took note of the way she handled the class discussions. When she mentioned a certain author or book she'd read, then I read it too.

I marvel now, that with Johanna's active family and other responsibilities, she still managed to find time for me. I rode in the car with her as she visited Sunday school members. We talked on the parking lot after church. Occasionally we walked along the country roads near her cabin on the lake and talked about everything from families to problem texts in Hebrews. In our discussions, my simple insights seemed to delight her just as her mature ones enthralled me. In short, Johanna embraced me as a friend—just as I was. Because she knew I looked up to her, she warned, "Don't imitate me, Gracie. Just be yourself and follow Jesus."

Today, when I think about my spiritual growth markers through the years, I can't help but think of Johanna. The relationship she had with me is the pattern I use as I mentor other women.

Nancy, a young woman in my Bible study group, called one day and asked, "Do you have time to help me?"

I found time by including her in my previously planned activities. "I usually go for a walk every morning at seven. Could you join me then?"

The next morning, Nancy's car pulled into my driveway just as I headed out the door in my tennis shoes. Twice a week for several months, we walked along the country roads near my house and talked about the Bible, our spiritual desires, our families.

One morning after walking, Nancy communicated the unmet longing of her heart: "I want to have children. Oh, Gracie, what if I never have them?" I promised to pray for her.

Imagine my joy when, a few months later, she called after a doctor's visit to say she was expecting a baby. Two years later she called again—with the same message. A couple of years after that, ditto. When I heard that third announcement I responded, "Whenever you're ready, I'll stop praying."

Another mentor in my life was an older woman named Mrs. Lenoir, who influenced me in a different way. Soon after I met her she invited me to visit and share fresh vegetables from her organically grown garden. Her simple lifestyle, emphasizing what really matters, caused me to rethink my priorities. As our friendship grew, I dropped by regularly to talk with her. Deep discussions took place in her kitchen as I watched her prepare vegetables for the freezer or knead the dough for her delicious whole-grain bread.

When I asked questions, Mrs. Lenoir answered, "I could tell you what I think, but I'd rather you come to your own conclusions. What does the Bible say, Gracie?" She gave me a concordance, and taught me to use an expository dictionary. Mrs. Lenoir talked with me about problems in her family and listened compassionately when I confessed some struggles of my own. "The Christian life is never easy," she explained, "Christians make wrong choices and often fail. Keep your eyes on the Lord."

I took Mrs. Lenoir's admonition to heart. So when, years later, I met a girl named Ashley, I wasn't shocked when she made a confession. "I'm pregnant," she sobbed. "My boyfriend deserted me, and my parents won't help. Even some of my Christian friends have turned their backs on me. I've lost my job. What can I do?" It was easy for me to love Ashley. I just loved her the way I'd been loved by women like Mrs. Lenoir and Johanna. Ashley and I worked to rebuild broken relationships in her family, and I supported her when she made plans to give the baby up for adoption. Our mentoring relationship continued during (and for years after) Ashley's crisis.

Eventually Ashley married a good man who loves her and loves her God. For several years they worked together in a private school for troubled teens. One day Ashley wrote, "Dear Gracie, I just wanted to write and thank you for loving me, forgiving me, and being my friend. We are so happy in the Lord. We are not making much money, but we are making a difference!"

The nice thing about mentoring others is that it doesn't demand a seminary degree or an ordained position in the church. All that's required is that a person be open, available, and ready to pour God's love into another life. Then, in time, the mentor will receive the blessing of watching that life go on to spread love to others, who spread love to others and—you get the incredible picture. It's a far-reaching, life-changing, eternal gift any ol' chicken—with nurturing wings—can give.

The older women . . . can train the younger women
to love their husbands and children,
to be self-controlled and pure, to be busy at home,
to be kind, and to be subject to their husbands,
so that no one will malign the word of God.
Titus 2:3-5

Famous Kindred Spirits

Quotes taken from *Always Friends* by
Alda Ellis, Harvest House Publishers,
Eugene, Oregon, 1997

Helen Keller and Anne Sullivan:

Helen wrote in her autobiography, "My teacher is so near
to me that I can scarcely think of myself apart from
her. . . . All the best of me belongs to her—there is not a
talent or an aspiration or a joy in me that has not been
awakened by her loving touch."

Elizabeth Barret Browning and Mary Russell Mitford:

Elizabeth wrote this expression of sympathy, "How my love
for you has been pulling at my sleeve these two days, to
write. . . . It haunts me that you are suffering. Believe, my
beloved friend, how near I am to you in thought, in prayer,
in sympathy of tender affection. I am alone; that is the
thought that clings to me, though when I think of you,
sister of my heart, it presses less heavily."

CHAPTER 40

Egg-niting the Gift Within

by Susan Duke

My good friend Cathy had no way of knowing that I'd stayed up most of the night, pecking away on a writing deadline that was slowly closing in on me when she asked me at lunch one day, "How do you really feel about writing? Is it all you hoped it would be?"

I was exhausted and my chicken-fried brain was taking the day off. Still, I pondered her question noting, with a smile, the excitement in her voice. Then carefully I answered, "I think there's this romantic notion floating around that a writer's life is filled with an unending progression of blissful and restful afternoons. People visualize writers sitting by a cozy fire, stirring a pot of winsome thoughts, then alternately dipping their feather pen into the inkwell of their soul. But let me tell you the truth: It's the hardest work I've ever done in my life."

My friend looked shocked, so I hastily added, "But it's also the most rewarding work I've ever done. And there really is a lot of dipping involved—into my soul, I mean."

As I typed out thoughts that had been accumulating for years, I felt as if I'd found a piece of my heart I didn't even know was missing. Still, if I didn't know with every fiber of my being this was something I was destined to do, I would quit today. After years of believing I would be a writer, I was still in for many a surprise when I finally got serious and dove in.

Perhaps, I postponed getting "serious" about writing because a part of me knew if I ever went beyond recording private thoughts and poetry in journals, my life would take a dramatic change. But I'll never forget the day when I knew it was time to step off of the sidelines and jump into writing with my whole heart.

It was in the spring of the year, and Harvey and I were driving through Arkansas and Missouri making stops for me to speak at several preset engagements. (My husband usually accompanies me on such long trips.) It was our first free afternoon in several days, and it felt wonderful to have some time to relax and do some sightseeing in the Ozark countryside. Someone suggested that we visit The Precious Moments Chapel in Carthage, Missouri, if we had the time. Since I've always loved the Precious Moments line of cards and giftware, I was anxious to take the advice.

The morning we arrived at The Precious Moments Chapel was sunny and warm. Harvey and I fell in line behind the tour group making its way down the stone path, then paused for a moment to survey the beautiful property surrounding the chapel. The endless rows of green hills gave us a feeling of remarkable tranquillity as we meandered our way to the chapel.

Stopping at the entrance, our tour guide told about the heavy wooden carved doors we were about to enter. "Every detail," she related, "has a special meaning." Upon entering the chapel, the tour guide let our group leisurely look around before starting her speech.

Everyone was obviously enamored by the heavenly scene of angels painted on the sky-blue ceiling. Special messages from children, in captions, adorned the walls.

While everyone else was busy taking photographs and chatting, I found myself becoming strangely emotional. Tears began to flow uncontrollably down my cheeks. I was desperately trying to stifle audible sobs. Quickly, I put my sunglasses back on, afraid someone would think I was one weird chick. Still, sunglasses couldn't hide the feelings that were gushing forth inside me. I wanted to lie down on the floor. I felt almost too weak to stand. I'd entered into a holy moment. A moment I will never forget. A moment that spoke so deeply to my soul, I knew when I walked out of those chapel doors I would never be quite the same again.

At first Harvey was so busy taking in the artwork, he didn't notice that I was a few steps behind him, falling apart. The more I tried to stop my runaway emotions, the more helpless I became. When Harvey finally turned around and saw me, he looked startled. I could see deep concern on his face as he reached for my hand. "Honey, what's wrong?"

"I can't . . . I just can't talk right now," I sobbed.

By now, the young tour guide had started her lecture. I managed to gain some composure but stayed as close to the back of the group as possible.

When the rest of the crowd finally moved on to another part of the chapel, I chose to stay behind. I knew mascara must have been all over my face, but a fresh stream of tears began to fall again. Harvey put his arms around me, silently wondering what this unusual display was about. I knew I had to offer him some sort of explanation, so I struggled to put into words what I was experiencing.

I'd always loved and admired the work of the Precious Moment's artist, Sam Butcher, but as I gazed upon the magnificent array of painted murals, my thoughts had begun focusing on the artist himself. Although Mr. Butcher had designed this chapel for sharing his art and giving joy to others, I kept envisioning the personal moments he spent working there. I wondered what he thought about as he lay on scaffolding, 32 feet in the air, painting angel after angel on the 1,500 square foot ceiling.

Behind the captivating paintings (all 5,000 square feet of them!), detailed with artistic splendor, I sensed the soul of a humble, sensitive, and—if I could venture a guess—private man. Finally, I found the words to express what I wanted to convey. It was a simple revelation, perhaps, but profound in its impact on me. I whispered to Harvey, "Do you see what I see? This man paints his heart. This is how he worships."

Now I knew why I felt as though I'd been walking on holy ground—because I had been.

This was more than a chapel someone had built for people to simply look at and admire.

Sure, that might be part of the purpose, but I suspected Sam Butcher spent many long nights here alone, prayerfully fulfilling, with every stroke of a brush, what God had called him to do. What began as a talent became a gift to the world and a form of worship to the Master Artist.

God used Sam Butcher's chapel to ignite a flame and motivate me to take the first steps toward becoming a real writer. I knew if Sam Butcher could "paint" his heart, God would help me find a way to "write" mine. For I believe, if God gives us a creative talent, we come to a point in our lives where we have no choice but to share it.

In that Precious Moments Chapel, I had my own precious moments. God helped me understand how He must feel when we let Him excavate a buried talent within us. An unused gift is like oil that sits in a lamp. Someone has to light the wick for the lamp to give off light. When we find the courage to bring our talents to light, it not only brings us satisfaction and peace, but God can use it to ignite a creative spark in others. For there are many "chicken souls" out there who are just waiting for someone to light their lamp with the flame of God's loving, creative heart.

> *Ye are the light of the world. A city that is set on an hill*
> *cannot be hid. Neither do men light a candle,*
> *and put it under a bushel, but on a candlestick;*
> *and it giveth light unto all that are in the house.*
> *Let your light so shine before men,*
> *that they may see your good works,*
> *and glorify your Father which is in heaven.*
> Matthew 5:14-16 KJV

Chicken Nugget

Pen from Heaven

Pen from heaven, write to me,
Words of what the Master sees.
Take my hand and let it flow
As a servant of my soul.

Pen from heaven, speak to me,
Oracles of sweet simplicity.
Take my laughter; take my pain,
And write for me of heaven's gain.

Pen from heaven, please impart
The words I need to write my heart.
From where celestial angels throng,
Pen from heaven, write the song.

Write the story, write the prose;
Write to me from where love grows.
Master author, closest friend,
Write to me from heaven's pen.

CHAPTER 41

Warming the Cackles of My Heart

by Susan Duke

A strange woman, wearing a red-plaid tattered robe and a head full of rollers held in place by a blue bandanna, entered the hush of the church sanctuary. Even her shoes were mismatched. Shocked expressions broke out on faces scattered about the room. As the woman came closer, it was impossible not to see the words on a hot pink button pinned to her robe. They read, "This is the earliest I've ever been late."

Who was this woman?

OK, I'll admit it. It was me.

Normally, it is important to me to present myself in a dignified manner. So why was I standing in church, in rollers and robe, looking so ridiculous?

It all began with an invitation from a local church to come teach a ladies' seminar on the biblical "motivational gifts." The night before the event, as I stood stirring some flour into a pan of sizzling butter, a crazy idea birthed itself somewhere in the right side of my brain: I would open the seminar with a visual aid these women would never forget.

In between adding salt, pepper, and milk to make gravy, my left brain began to protest.

After all, Susan, you've never done anything quite this wild before. Don't you want that group to know you are serious about the ministry of teaching and speaking? And what about that quiet, worshipful song you'd planned to sing? Dare you open a "deep, teaching seminar" with a ridiculous stunt?

What can I say? My crazy right brain loves a dare. Ideas were coming as fast as I could stir the gravy. My left brain was speechless.

As I sat a hearty fried chicken dinner on the table, I couldn't wait to share my ideas with my husband Harvey—to tell him about the props and costumes I'd pull together to make an unforgettable point. He gave an "I don't know about this" response, mingled with a "surely-you've-got-to-be-kidding" raise of his eyebrows. I almost reconsidered.

But it was too late. My right brain was, at this point, on a full-fledged roll. Harvey's reluctance only added fuel to my wildfire. There would be no stopping me now!

The next morning, after kissing me good-bye, my husband shook his head in bewilderment as he watched his robed n' rolled wife walk out to the car. Under his breath I could hear him moan, "Mercy, mercy, mercy."

I looked up and winked at him before ducking into the car, "You've got it, Harvey—that's another one of the motivational gifts I'll be talking about today!"

He uttered a spontaneous prayer—something like, "Lord, please don't let my wife's car break down while she's running around in that get-up."

As soon as I arrived at the church, I cornered the pastor's wife and asked her to simply introduce me, then pause and wait for me to come in. "When I don't come in right away," I explained, "just introduce me again. I'll take it from there." Several minutes and several introductions later, I came sailing into the gathering, breathlessly, amidst gasps and chuckles from the audience.

"While preparing this teaching," I began saying as I fumbled for the microphone, alternately dropping and picking up my notes, "I discovered that one gift I don't have is the gift of organization. However, I am working on it." With that, I reached inside an enormous flowered purse and pulled out a calendar/organizer the size of a small country. Talk about your "day-at-a-glance!"

The calendar was followed by a dog leash, packets of Sweet and Low, assorted matches, an "emergency" pair of pantyhose, a magnifying glass, a coffee filter, crayons, a hot glue gun, a tape measurer, ear muffs and a small *New Testament*. Soon the room was filled with undignified howls of laughter. Mission accomplished.

I exited, asking for a five minute break, so I could don proper dress and regain my composure. When I returned, we got down to business and the *spiritual* purpose for the meeting. All day long, I was amazed at the enthusiasm and open spirits of the women who had come. It wasn't until after the meeting, while saying my good-byes, that I understood why the humorous prelude had been so well-received.

"You have no idea how much we needed to laugh today," the pastor's wife said. "We've been through some terrible trials lately, it felt like sadness and anger had almost taken up residence in our church home. Things had gotten so bad, I'd even thought about canceling today's seminar. I certainly wasn't expecting what happened today, but I am so glad God knew what we needed."

C. S. Lewis said, "Joy is the serious business of heaven." This truth is a soft pillow to our heavy souls.

I once heard someone say, "Only when you experience the depths of great grief, can you truly understand great joy."

I have experienced a grief so deep, I once feared it would hold me forever in its insolent grip. Losing my beloved 18-year-old son, Thomas, tragically and suddenly in a car accident, sent me reeling into an abyss of darkness. There was no foreseeable joy in my future.

When grief strikes its formidable blow upon our lives, all of us are left wondering if we will ever again know even a semblance of joy. I believed God could comfort me, even give me peace. But joy? That seemed impossible. Before tragedy came into our home, the undergirding motive behind everything I did was to encourage and bring joy to others. I thought bringing joy was what God had called me to do with my life. After Thomas' death, that sort of ministry seemed lost to me forever.

But even when I didn't feel it, some small dying ember in my soul clung to the words of the Psalmist, "Weeping may endure for a night, but joy comes in the morning" (Psalm 30:5 AMP).

Then very slowly, one step and one day at a time, God began to send a bucket of hope to the well of my soul. Yes, I had been forever changed by the loss of my child, but eventually, I began embracing life with a whole new perspective.

I discovered that joy, after a great time of grief, ultimately comes down to a choice. At a certain point in time, I determined I would not only allow God to restore joy to my life, I would invite Him to bring it in deeper and fuller measures than ever before. "They who sow in tears," wrote the Psalmist, "shall reap in joy and singing."

If you happen to be going through a trial that's taken all the joy from your life—take it from one whose mother hen heart was once shattered, and still has tender pain-filled places: what God says is true. In His time, joy and singing will come knocking again.

But it's up to you to invite them in.

> *He will yet fill your mouth with laughter . . .*
> *and your lips with joyful shouting.*
> Job 8:21 AMP

Choose Joy

Chicken Nugget

> At the crossroads of life's journey,
> When my heart had lost its song,
> When darkness overwhelmed me,
> When I felt anything but strong,
> I heard my faint heart whisper,
> You will have joy again.
> God will mend your broken heart
> He's your healer and your friend,
> And His joy will be your strength,
> But your heart must make the choice
> And when you do, you will find
> Heaven's reasons to rejoice.

Meet the Authors

Becky Freeman's full nest consists of her husband of 21 years, Scott, and four chicks, ages 11-18. Her brood supplied much of the material for her books which include *Adult Children of Fairly Functional Parents, Worms in My Tea and Other Mixed Blessings* (a Gold Medallion Finalist), *Marriage 9-1-1, Still Lickin' the Spoon,* and *A View from the Porch Swing.* Becky has been interviewed on more than 200 radio stations and appeared on television shows such as *Good Morning, Texas, The Crook and Chase Show,* ABC's *Caryl and Marilyn* ("The Mommies") Show, *100 Huntley Street Open Home Show,* Ontario's *City TV,* and *Home Life Television Show.* She also writes the popular "Marriage 9-1-1" column for *Home Life Magazine.*

Becky has been a first grade teacher, a food caterer, and a newspaper columnist—all experiences contributing to the humorous stories in her books.

Susan Duke is a wife, mother, grandmother, freelance writer, speaker, and singer. For 12 years Susan has ministered in Christian conferences, women's retreats, correctional facilities, youth rallies, seminars, and churches of all denominations through her own "Heartsong Ministries." She was praise and worship leader in an interdenominational women's group, has recorded several Gospel albums, and writes Gospel music, psalms, and poetry.

Susan's work has appeared in publications such as *Home Life, The Greenville Herald Banner,* and *The Cross and the Quill.* She makes her nest in a quaint log cabin, built by her husband Harvey, and designed with the same flair that hatched her antique and decorating business years ago. She has been married for 22 years.

Rebecca Barlow Jordan has published more than 1,500 greeting cards, poems, articles, newspaper columns and numerous calendars including the 365-day *In His Image*. Her works have appeared in *Focus on the Family, Discipleship Journal, Home Life, Family Circle, Marriage Partnership,* and others. She co-authored, *Marriage Toners: Weekly Exercises to Strengthen Your Relationship* with her husband of 31 years, Larry, who is an associate pastor.

Rebecca speaks at writers' workshops and women's events and helps lead marriage enrichment classes. She has been a deaf interpreter and taught Bible studies for more than 25 years. She is a mother hen at rest in her emptied nest—two grown daughters, one married.

Gracie Malone is a freelance writer, Bible study teacher, and speaker at conferences and retreats. For more than 25 years, she has mentored women, developed leaders, and established small group ministries. Her articles have been published in *Discipleship Journal, Moody, Christian Parenting Today, Home Life, Women Alive,* and others. She has also received the "Best Article" Award at Florida's Christian Writer's Conference.

She and her husband Joe, who is an engineer for IBM, have been married for 35 years. They have three sons and five grandchicks.

Fran Caffey Sandin is the author of *See You Later, Jeffrey,* and contributed a chapter in *The Strength of a Woman*. Fran's numerous articles have appeared in *Moody, Virtue, Focus on the Family Physician, Home Life, Journal of Christian Nursing, The Christian Medical Society Journal,* and *The Joyful Woman*.

Fran is a registered nurse and works for James, her physician husband of 33 years. She is an organist in her church, co-directs women's ministries, and teaches a young couples' class with her husband. They have three children: a single rooster, a married hen, and their youngest chick waiting for them in heaven.

Additional copies of this
book are available
from your local bookstore.

Honor Books
Tulsa, Oklahoma